J. K. ROWLING
BEHIND THE MAGIC

TRAILBLAZERS

Neil Armstrong

Jackie Robinson

Harriet Tubman

Jane Goodall

Albert Einstein

Beyoncé

Stephen Hawking

Simone Biles

Martin Luther King Jr.

J. K. Rowling

>>TRAILBLAZERS

J. K. ROWLING
BEHIND THE MAGIC

CATH SENKER

RANDOM HOUSE 🏠 NEW YORK

Text copyright © 2020 by Cath Senker
Cover art copyright © 2020 by Luisa Uribe
Interior illustrations copyright © 2020 by Tom Heard

Visit us on the Web! rhcbooks.com

Educators and librarians, for a variety of teaching tools,
visit us at RHTeachersLibrarians.com

Library of Congress Cataloging-in-Publication Data is available upon request.
ISBN 978-0-593-12461-1 (trade pbk.)—ISBN 978-0-593-12462-8 (lib. bdg.)—
ISBN 978-0-593-12463-5 (ebook)

Created by Stripes Publishing Limited, an imprint of the Little Tiger Group

Printed in the United States of America
10 9 8 7 6 5 4 3 2 1
First Edition

Contents

INTRODUCTION

A MAGICAL MOMENT

On Friday, July 21, 2007, a long line of little witches and wizards were waiting for the clock to strike midnight. They had been outside a Barnes & Noble store in New York City for hours, clutching their wands. Younger ones were napping in sleeping bags while older fans discussed popular Harry Potter characters, played games, and munched snacks. Something magical was about to happen.

⋛ STROKE OF MIDNIGHT ⋚

The doors to the bookstore swung open, and there it was: *Harry Potter and the Deathly Hallows*, the final volume of the series. Cheers rippled down the line, and elated children entered the shop one by one to purchase their copies. A journey of discovery awaited every reader. What would happen in the final showdown between seventeen-year-old Harry Potter and his mortal enemy, Voldemort?

In cities around the world, as the clock chimed midnight in each time zone, bookstores opened their doors for launch parties—a tradition that had started with the launch of *Harry Potter and the Goblet of Fire* in 2000. An estimated 800,000 people worldwide celebrated the publication of their new favorite book at a store. And then, arriving home in the early hours, they climbed into bed and began to read, desperate to learn how the adventure would end.

July 22, 2007

THE NEW YORK TIMES

RECORD-BREAKING BOOK SALES

Eleven million copies of *Harry Potter and the Deathly Hallows* sell within 24 hours.

≍ HARRY POTTER MAGIC ≍

So why were thousands of children lining up at bookstores at midnight dressed as Harry, Hermione, and Ron? The enormous crowds that gathered outside stores worldwide were there because of one special writer: J. K. Rowling. She had created the magic of Harry Potter, which had captured readers' imaginations in a way few books did at the turn of the twenty-first century. Over ten years, J. K. Rowling had worked fast and furiously to bring out a new volume almost every year. Young people— and adults, too—rushed to grab each new book in the series the moment it was published. Children who had never before been interested in reading were racing through her thick books and passing them along to their friends. Everyone was talking about the boy wizard.

Fantasy Worlds

Of course, popular children's fantasy books had existed before. In the 1930s and 1940s, British author J. R. R. Tolkien wrote *The Hobbit* and *The Lord of the Rings*. In *The Lord of the Rings*, various peoples of Middle Earth—among them dwarves, men, elves, and hobbits—are drawn into a struggle to destroy a magic ring and overcome the power of the evil Lord Sauron.

Later, many children grew up with the Narnia series by C. S. Lewis, published in the 1950s. Like the Harry Potter series, the Chronicles of Narnia comprise seven books in which children visit a hidden

realm with talking animals and magic. In the bestselling title of the series, *The Lion, the Witch and the Wardrobe,* four children living in a dusty old country

house discover a wardrobe that is a gateway to the magical land of Narnia. Similarly, in the Harry Potter books, the invisible barrier at Platform 9¾ at King's Cross station leads students into a parallel world.

The Narnia books and *The Lord of the Rings* became classics and were still popular in the 1990s. But children were reading less than those of earlier generations did. A wider variety of entertainment, from TV to movies to video games, was available. Teachers worried that children were less interested in reading than in other activities. The time was ripe for a new generation of fantasy stories. Yet becoming the next Tolkien or C. S. Lewis would not be easy.

Looking at Joanne Rowling in the mid-1990s, it was difficult to believe she would become that author. She was a single mother caring for her daughter, Jessica. Many single parents with young children lived in poverty then, and still do today. Unless they have friends or family members to help look after their children, it is very difficult for single parents to get a job. Some are able to work from home, but raising children takes a lot of time and energy, so the parent has little spare time.

In the United Kingdom, single parents who cannot go out to work receive some welfare benefits—a small sum of money from the government for rent, bills, and food. Joanne had to survive on those benefits.

With little money, Joanne could afford only the basics. She and Jessica lived in a tiny apartment in Edinburgh, Scotland. It was cramped, cold, and uncomfortable, and Joanne could not bear to stay at home. Every day, she took Jessica out and scribbled the story of Harry Potter in a café while her baby napped. How could she ever have imagined she would be the first novelist to become a billionaire?

⊰ ORPHAN HARRY ⊱

Harry Potter's tale begins during summer vacation when he is eleven years old and, like most other British children, preparing to put on a new uniform and go to the local public school. But unlike many others, Harry is an orphan, living with his uncle and aunt and his cousin Dudley, who see him as an unwanted burden. However, Harry is no ordinary boy existing in the normal world of the non-magical people, or Muggles. He is a wizard, born to witch and wizard parents who were murdered when he was a baby. Harry is invited to join Hogwarts School of Witchcraft and Wizardry, where he learns about the secret parallel world of magical beings, displays a natural talent for the sport of Quidditch, and makes friends for the first time in his life. His friends include Hermione Granger, who is highly intelligent, and Ron Weasley, one of the youngest of a large wizarding family, who is living in the shadow of his elder siblings. The trio become embroiled in challenges and adventures far outside the wizarding curriculum.

HOGWARTS HOUSES

At boarding school, Harry, Ron, and Hermione get to know each other because they are in the same house, Gryffindor. Many schools in the United Kingdom divide students into houses that compete against each other in sports and other activities. J. K. Rowling devised four Hogwarts houses, each with its own character. A magic Sorting Hat separates the young witches and wizards, assigning each to the house that best suits their personality on arrival. The students live in their house dormitories, attend many of their lessons together, and form deep and lasting friendships.

GRYFFINDOR
courage,
bravery,
determination

SLYTHERIN
ambition,
cunning

HUFFLEPUFF
patience,
loyalty,
hard work

RAVENCLAW
learning,
humor

⋛ BREAKING THE RULES ⋚

To outsiders, the publishing world might seem as hard to
enter as Hogwarts School is for Muggles. Getting your
first novel in print is a complicated business. Publishers
have ideas about what kind of story will work, and
authors need to present the right kind of tale at the right
time. Joanne had heard that children's authors should
avoid male heroes and that adventures set in boarding
schools were unfashionable. They had been popular
earlier in the twentieth century but now felt out-of-date.
Children's books were usually short; writers tried to make
sure they were no longer than 45,000 words.

J. K. Rowling broke all those rules. For her, boarding school was the ideal setting for her boy hero's story about friendship—and the first volume was nearly 77,000 words long.

The truth is that I found success by stumbling off alone in a direction most people thought was a dead end.

CHAPTER 1

A BORN STORYTELLER

Joanne's mother and father met on a long train trip when they were just eighteen years old. Anne Volant and Peter Rowling were traveling from King's Cross in London to Arbroath in Scotland. By chance, they had both recently joined the British navy. The pair hit it off, and they talked and talked on the nine-hour train journey. Their relationship blossomed, and a year later they decided to give up navy life, get married, and settle down.

Peter and Anne moved into a house in Yate, a small town near Bristol, England, where Peter soon found a job in an aircraft factory making engines for fighter planes. In 1965, Joanne was born. Her sister, Dianne— known as Di—followed in 1967. Joanne remembers the birth of her sister, even though she was barely two years old at the time.

My dad gave me Play-Doh the day [Di] arrived, to keep me occupied while he ran in and out of the bedroom. I have no memory of seeing the new baby, but I do remember eating the Play-Doh.

Although Joanne came into the world in Yate, she often says she was born in nearby Chipping Sodbury, because it has a more interesting name. A pretty medieval town, Chipping Sodbury is full of beautiful buildings, antiques stores, and lovely homes. In contrast, few people have heard of Yate, even though it has existed for more than a thousand years.

When Harry Potter visits his parents' gravestones, we learn that he, like his creator, was born to 20-year-old parents.

When Joanne was four, the Rowling family moved to a bigger home with three bedrooms in the village of Winterbourne, near Bristol. Here, the growing girls would have more space to play. It was a friendly neighborhood. The factories around Bristol attracted workers from many parts of the United Kingdom.

Anne had given up her navy career to get married and have a family. In the United Kingdom in 1961, about one-third of married women worked outside the home. It was common for a woman to leave her job when she had a baby. Women often returned to work once their children were older—as Anne later did.

<u>The Swinging Sixties</u>

The late 1960s were a time of considerable cultural change in the United Kingdom, the United States, and other countries. Bands such as the Beatles and the Rolling Stones were revolutionizing the music industry, and young people wore daring new fashions: brightly colored clothes, tiny miniskirts, and widely flared, or bell-bottom, jeans. Some people were inspired to become involved in social movements—for example, campaigning against nuclear weapons or against the US involvement in the Vietnam War. Even Joanne's parents, in their small village, were influenced by the new culture. They loved dancing to Beatles records in their living room.

AN IMAGINATIVE GIRL

Peter and Anne enjoyed reading, and their home was full of books. They always read to the girls at bedtime. Joanne especially loved fantasy and classic books. When she was four, she caught the measles and was stuck in bed for days. Her dad read Kenneth Grahame's *The Wind in the Willows* to her, with tales of the animal characters Rat, Mole, Toad, and Badger, who live in the English countryside and go on adventures.

From an early age, Joanne adored inventing her own stories, too, and used to tell them to her little sister. She wrote her first tale when she was six, called "Rabbit and Miss Bee." Her family always praised her creative spirit.

"Ever since 'Rabbit and Miss Bee,' I knew I wanted to be a writer." —J. K. Rowling

Animal Friends

Animals would later play a big part in the Harry Potter stories. All the students at Hogwarts are allowed to bring an animal with them—an owl, cat, toad, or rat is permitted. But like the animals in Joanne's childhood storybooks, these creatures are not merely pets; they take an active role in the students' adventures. Owls carry letters between students and the outside world, while Ron's rat and Hermione's cat have their own missions.

⋛ MAKE-BELIEVE GAMES ⋛

Joanne and Di spent many happy hours playing around the village with their friends, including siblings Ian and Vikki Potter. Some people think the character of Harry Potter is based on Ian, but Joanne says she simply liked his last name.

Imaginative games were their favorite, and the children loved dressing up as different characters. Anne kept a dress-up box full of old clothes for them to create their outfits. Joanne was usually in charge. In her games, often the girls were witches and the boys were wizards. She invented spells, and they pretended to make disgusting potions in a cauldron. The children borrowed their parents' brooms so they could pretend to fly around their invented world.

"Joanne would always make up spells and things and stories where we'd all be the characters." —Ian Potter

⋛ FAMILY FEASTS ⋛

When Joanne was young, people could not buy premade meals in a supermarket, and there were few takeout restaurants. Occasionally, families might go out for fish and chips or burgers, but only as a rare treat. Anne Rowling bought fresh vegetables and fruit from the grocery store, and every evening she prepared a traditional English dinner. She was a great cook. When Peter came back from work, the family sat around the table to eat a delicious meal together.

Joanne and Di celebrated their birthdays at home, too. Anne would make a tray of sandwiches, and when the girls had gobbled them up, they enjoyed Jell-O with ice cream, and little cupcakes.

Then they turned out the lights, and Anne came in with a beautiful home-baked cake with lighted candles for the birthday girl to blow out and make a wish.

The Hogwarts Menu

Later, when writing the Harry Potter books, Joanne often described the wonderful food at Hogwarts—always popular English dishes, and plenty of them. At his first Hogwarts meal, Harry is awestruck to see beef, chicken, pork chops, sausages, bacon, and more, served alongside fries and boiled and roasted potatoes. After the hearty main course, a selection of desserts instantly arrives: fruit, doughnuts, cakes, pies, puddings—and strawberries for anyone too full for anything else. Every meal is a feast that magically appears on the tables.

⋛ LIFE IN TUTSHILL ⋜

In 1974, when Joanne was nine, the family moved again.
Their new home was Tutshill, a village in the Forest of
Dean, Gloucestershire. Here, the girls lived a country
life in a farming area on the edge of the forest. They
moved into Church Cottage, next door to the village
school. Joanne and Di would have no excuse for being
late to class in the morning!

Jo's teacher was Mrs. Sylvia Morgan, who she thought
was strict and scary. On the first day of school, Mrs.
Morgan gave the class a math test on fractions, which
Joanne had not yet learned. Joanne did extremely badly
and was put in a row with others who had failed the test.
Though she was upset, Joanne refused to cry in front of
her classmates, instead becoming determined to move
from that row.

The Three Rs

Sylvia Morgan was a traditional teacher,
who believed in focusing on the three Rs:
→ reading
→ writing
→ arithmetic
She taught her students by making them
memorize information for tests.

Joanne studied hard and got better grades on the weekly tests in all subjects. By the end of the year, Mrs. Morgan had moved her to sit with the high-scoring students.

≥ FUN AND GAMES ≤

As a schoolgirl, Joanne was shy and serious. She wore thick glasses, loved reading, and was not very confident. Her sister, Di, was more lively and outgoing.

Joanne and Di loved visiting their father's mother, Grandma Kathleen, and her husband, Ernie. The couple ran a grocery shop. If it was quiet and there were no customers, the children were allowed to play "store" using real groceries, and weigh out candy.

When Joanne was nine, Kathleen died at the age of fifty-two. Joanne had been close to her grandmother and was hit with great sadness. She learned very young that dealing with death is a natural part of everyone's life.

In 1975, Joanne joined the Brownies, a club for girls, and her sister signed up not long after. They met every week to learn skills such as sewing, cooking, and first aid and to help out with community projects. The Brown Owl (the leader of the Brownie pack), Sylvia Lewis, remembers how different the two girls were—Di bouncy and laughing, and Joanne rather sensible and more responsible.

⇒ SECRET AMBITION ⇐

Joanne always loved books—her parents allowed her to read anything she wanted. She also practiced writing and was always scribbling stories. One was called "The Seven Cursed Diamonds," about seven diamonds and the people who owned them. But she did not tell anyone that she secretly dreamed of becoming a writer.

Joanne absorbed ideas from the books she read. She was influenced by the children's author E. Nesbit, who wrote *The Railway Children*. The classic book tells the story of three children and their mother, who are forced to move to a simple cottage by a railroad station after their father is mysteriously taken away. The children have exciting adventures, including preventing a train disaster, while remaining haunted by the disappearance of their father. Children missing parents and saving the day: these themes would be key to Joanne's future writing.

C. S. Lewis's Narnia books appealed greatly to Jo, too. The magical world of Narnia, full of extraordinary talking creatures, clearly influenced her, but she would go on to develop her imaginative universe in her own unique way.

Joanne's Bedtime Reading

These books had a powerful impact on
Joanne as she was growing up.

→ Books by Noel Streatfeild, particularly *Ballet
Shoes*, a story about three adopted sisters
who win places at a dance school and become
child performers.

→ *The Story of the Treasure Seekers* by
E. Nesbit. Like *The Railway Children*, the
treasure seekers are young people who try to
save the day. After their mother dies, the six
Bastable children attempt to recover their
father's fortune.

→ *The Little White Horse* by Elizabeth Goudge.
Maria is a 13-year-old orphan who has to
leave behind her life in London for a strange
and different place in the countryside. The
book has long, detailed descriptions of
magnificent feasts.

CHAPTER 2

FROM SHYNESS TO POPULARITY

In the United Kingdom, starting secondary school at eleven years old is a major life change. Luckily, Joanne went with nearly all her classmates from Tutshill to her new school, Wyedean Comprehensive. The students were the children of rural families or newcomers drawn to the region for work.

Joanne was an eager student, always the first to raise her hand in class. She did well at school, especially in English and languages. Her English classes read William Golding's *Lord of the Flies,* about a group of schoolboys stranded on an island, and *Walkabout* by James Vance Marshall, a tale of two American children who are lost in the Australian desert and are helped by a local Aboriginal boy.

Outside school, Joanne chose to read more complex novels, including classics by the nineteenth-century author Jane Austen, which she still enjoys today. These books feature strong female characters. Yet Joanne also loved exciting adventure stories, such as the James Bond novels by Ian Fleming.

Education for All

In the 1970s, most British children went to their local comprehensive, a public school with no entrance exams or fees to pay. Comprehensive schools provided the opportunity for all children to work hard, achieve good grades, and maybe apply to university. In the Harry Potter books, Hogwarts is a public school, open to all witches and wizards, whether they are from a rich or a poor background. But unlike most public schools, Hogwarts is a boarding school, and Joanne admits that she never wanted to go to boarding school herself.

A Knack for Names

Joanne was always fascinated by peculiar names of people and places, and the sound of words and the feelings they summon up. She stored them in her memory to use in her stories. The name Hermione comes from a character in Shakespeare's *The Winter's Tale*, Dumbledore is an old word for a bumblebee, and Snape is a village on the Suffolk coast in eastern England. Joanne also likes inventing names—she made up Quidditch.

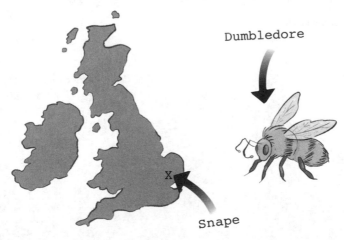

Dumbledore

Snape

⋛ A BUDDING WRITER ⋜

Jo's favorite teacher was Lucy Shepherd, who taught English. Ever enthusiastic, Lucy supported her students to develop their creative side. She was also a feminist—she believed that girls should have the same opportunities that boys do, and she always encouraged girls to study hard. She inspired Joanne to do some creative writing. Joanne said, "English was easily my best subject, but she wasn't about to tell me how brilliant I was. She pushed me to do better, which is what I needed." Joanne was still not ready to admit—even to her favorite teacher—that she dreamed of being a writer.

"As a writer, you should structure your work and make sure you pace your story so it moves neither too quickly nor too slowly." —Lucy Shepherd, Joanne's English teacher

⋛ STANDING UP FOR HERSELF ⋚

School had its downsides. Joanne was not particularly gifted at science. Her chemistry teacher was John Nettleship, who was known by the students as "Stinger"—probably because his name made them think of stinging nettles, a common weed in the United Kingdom that causes a painful sting. Some of his students, including Joanne, used to feel that he singled them out to answer questions. Joanne's impression of teachers like "Stinger" may have shaped the character of Snape, who always picks on Harry in class, hoping he will fail to answer and be humiliated.

Wearing her thick glasses, Joanne was seen as serious and nerdy, and sometimes other students bullied her. She was forced to learn to stand up for herself. Once, a larger girl attacked her, and Joanne felt forced to fight back. "For a few days I was quite famous, because she hadn't managed to flatten me," Joanne recalled. When Joanne started writing the Harry Potter books, she resolved to create a hero who wore glasses, alongside a nerdy, hardworking companion.

> "It wasn't the coolest thing to be too bright at my school. I was a bit of a Hermione."
> —J. K. Rowling

⋚ ANNE ROWLING'S ILLNESS ⋚

Once her daughters were at secondary school and did not need her around during the day, Joanne's mother, Anne, took a job at Wyedean as a lab assistant. She helped prepare the materials and equipment for the students' science lessons. Some students might be embarrassed to have their parent working at their school, but Anne and her daughters got along exceedingly well. She was fun to be with and had a great sense of humor. The three walked to school and back each day, chatting and laughing together.

When Joanne was fourteen, her mother became ill. One of the first signs was that Anne's hand started to shake when she was pouring tea. After a year of seemingly endless hospital tests, she was told she had multiple sclerosis. With her bright, positive attitude, Anne continued to work and enjoy her normal hobbies, including playing the guitar. On good days she could carry out her daily tasks, but on bad days she had difficulty walking. It was distressing for Joanne to see the effects of her mother's illness.

Increasingly, the bad days outnumbered the good ones, and Anne gradually became less able to perform everyday activities. She could no longer reliably hold test tubes in the lab, so she regretfully gave up her job at the school. Anne did her best to stay active, even though walking took supreme effort. She used to clean the church next door to her home, just to keep busy and be useful. But despite Anne's cheerful outlook, life became more and more challenging for her—and for her family, too. For Jo, witnessing her mother's pain and sadness made home "a difficult place to be." She knew that her mother would never recover and didn't want to think too much about the future.

What Is Multiple Sclerosis (MS)?

MS is a lifelong condition that affects the central nervous system. This disease occurs when the immune system mistakenly attacks and damages tissue in the brain or spinal cord. It can sometimes cause serious disability, although its symptoms can occasionally be mild.

MS symptoms include:

→ tiredness

→ difficulty walking

→ impaired balance and coordination

→ vision problems

There is no cure for MS, but various treatments can help control the symptoms.

⋛ OUT AND ABOUT IN THE FOREST ⋚

Young people living near the Forest of Dean complained that it was boring there, with not much to do. Sometimes Joanne and her friends went to a nearby youth club to play games and meet others. The closest town was Chepstow, but it had little going on—there wasn't even a movie theater. To see the newly released movie *Grease* in 1978, Joanne and her friends had to travel twelve miles (19 kilometers) to the movie theater in Coleford. But at least Chepstow had a disco, where they could dance to tracks from *Saturday Night Fever.*

In her late teens, Joanne began listening to punk music—the Clash was one of her favorite bands. Joanne wore heavy black eye makeup like Siouxsie Sioux from the band Siouxsie and the Banshees.

West Country Magic

Although the teenaged Joanne found the social life in the Forest of Dean dull, its history and traditions fed her active imagination. Stories of witchcraft and magic abounded, including the legend of a man who could turn into an animal. Many a plot twist in the Harry Potter tale starts with an animal that is not quite as it seems. And Hagrid, one of the best-loved characters, speaks with a strong West Country accent.

⋛ DARING TO BE DIFFERENT ⋚

School became an escape from the stress of home life and her mother's illness. At sixteen, Joanne chose English, French, and German for her A levels, the exams she needed to take so she could apply for university. She developed a love for Shakespeare's plays after going on a trip to the world-famous theater in Stratford-upon-Avon, the playwright's hometown, to watch a performance of *King Lear*.

By her final year at Wyedean, Joanne had become far more outgoing and popular, and she became head girl—the girl selected as a student leader and representative of the school. She developed an interest in global issues, supporting Greenpeace, which aimed to protect the environment, and the human rights organization Amnesty International. That year, she made friends with Sean Harris, a new classmate at school. He was the first of her friends to learn to drive and was lucky enough to have a car. Their world expanded as they went on trips to cities around the area, including Bristol, Bath, Newport, and Cardiff, going to clubs and shows. Comfortable in her friend's company, Joanne confided in Sean her secret ambition to be a writer.

The Magic Ford Anglia

Sean Harris drove a turquoise Ford Anglia—a car that would later feature in *Harry Potter and the Chamber of Secrets*. Enhanced by magic so it can fly and become invisible, the car is used by the Weasley brothers to rescue Harry from his horrible family.

JESSICA MITFORD

Joanne became interested in politics and social issues, inspired by writers such as Jessica Mitford. Jessica had been raised in a wealthy family that had little tolerance for people with views that differed from its own. Despite this upbringing, Jessica decided to follow her own path. She ran away to Spain and married a man who had traveled there to fight in the Spanish Civil War. She later moved to the United States and wrote books about human rights issues, such as problems in the prison system.

⌇ OFF TO UNIVERSITY ⌇

Joanne was a talented, ambitious student. In her final year at Wyedean, she set her sights high, applying for a place at the top-ranked University of Oxford. Even though her grades were good enough, she was rejected. It was extremely hard for students from public schools to secure a place at Oxford or Cambridge. Every year, one or two students from Wyedean would apply, but it was rare for them to be accepted.

Disappointed, Joanne decided to stay in the West of England to study. In the summer of 1983, she accepted a place at the University of Exeter, in Devon, to study French and German. She had been hoping to study English literature, but her parents thought languages would be more valuable for finding a job afterward. Joanne found she was not well suited to studying languages and soon dropped German for classics, keeping the decision quiet from her parents to avoid an argument. In classics, she would study the history, language, books, and stories of ancient Rome and Greece.

Although Joanne was fascinated by the myths and legends of the ancient world, the classics courses did not inspire her greatly, and she was an average student in French. Because she was not enthusiastic about her studies, she did not work hard and sometimes missed classes or even lost her work. Joanne was a daydreamer, always thinking up stories—and she still had a passion for writing. Perhaps she would have been a more eager student had she chosen to study English.

⋛ STUDENT STORIES ⋚

Like most new students, Joanne was eager to make friends and have fun. She had completely shaken off her nerdy image, now dressing in long, flouncy skirts with a jean jacket. Joanne and her group of new friends could often be found drinking coffee in the Devonshire House café at the university or going to the Black Horse pub in Exeter. As she had done as a child, Joanne invented stories for her university friends, in which they were the characters. Music also remained important to her: she was a fan of the Smiths and tried to play the band's songs on the guitar.

Joanne's time in Exeter influenced the people and places in the Harry Potter books. In *Harry Potter and the Philosopher's Stone,* the 665-year-old Nicolas Flamel lives in the city. It is thought that Joanne based the fictional Diagon Alley on Gandy Street in Exeter. A quaint narrow lane with cobblestones and no cars, it is lined with old-fashioned stores. There are little clothes shops, jewelers, and cafés. On the corner of Gandy Street stands the Vaults bar, which looks very much like Gringotts Bank in the Harry Potter books.

Joanne often forgot to return her books to the university library on time. Patrons did not receive warnings to renew their books back in the 1980s, and so poor Joanne ran up a library fine of £50—about $150 today.

⫽ A YEAR IN PARIS ⫽

As part of her university studies, Joanne spent her third year in Paris, which was a great opportunity to improve her French, learn about the culture, and meet international students. She shared an apartment with an Italian man, a Spanish woman, and a Russian woman. Jo's job was to teach English at a school in Paris, and by mixing with French people at work and living in the city, she learned to speak French fluently. In her spare time, she continued to read and write stories. Joanne did not get along with her Italian roommate and would often hide away in her room reading English classics, simply to avoid him. While in Paris, she spent whole days reading Charles Dickens novels and *The Lord of the Rings*.

The Lord of the Rings and the Harry Potter Books

Fantasy tales frequently describe entire worlds and feature a battle between good and evil. Though these two works are very different from each other, they have some similar elements.

CHARACTER OR FEATURE	*THE LORD OF THE RINGS*	HARRY POTTER SERIES
Dark Lord	Sauron	Voldemort
Significant wizard leader	Gandalf	Dumbledore
Black-cloaked beings that create terror and despair	Ringwraiths	Dementors
Mirror for visions	Mirror of Galadriel (shows visions of the past, present, and future)	Mirror of Erised (shows the deepest desire of the viewer)
Giant venomous spider	Shelob	Aragog

≳ FUN AND FINALS ≲

Once back at the University of Exeter, the students who had spent a year abroad hung out together. Joanne liked going to bars and parties, and she started going out with a new boyfriend. In her final year, she became involved with putting on a French play and wrote her 3,000-word dissertation (a long essay on a topic the student chooses) in French. She spent many hours in the library and studied enough to pass her exams and get her degree. Joanne graduated in 1987, achieving a decent grade but not one that would help her find a good job.

Meanwhile, back at home, Joanne's mother was getting sicker. When Joanne's proud parents attended her graduation ceremony, Anne was in a wheelchair.

CHAPTER 3

THE WORLD OF WORK

After graduation, Joanne needed to find a job. It did not even enter her head to try to get her stories published. Since she wasn't really sure what she wanted to do, she took a secretarial course for people with language skills. She moved to London and found a position as a temp—a temporary office worker sent to different companies when required. Joanne has said she was a "nightmare" as a secretary; she was not well organized and found it hard to focus on her tasks. Yet she learned to type quickly, a skill that in time would prove extremely useful.

Now, where has that letter gone?

Send in the Secretary

Computers were rare in offices in the 1980s, so secretaries were hired to type all the documents. Senior staff did not write their own letters but instead told their secretaries what to write, and the secretaries typed the letters for them to sign. At that time, the role was generally seen as a woman's job.

Joanne drifted from job to job as a secretary. She also worked as a researcher for Amnesty International for two years, helping investigate human rights abuses in French-speaking African countries. Joanne heard heartrending stories of brave people living under brutal governments who had been captured and tortured for speaking out. It was difficult hearing about such terrible experiences. At lunchtime, she would leave her desk and speed off to a pub or café, where she'd work on two novels for adults. But neither was ever published, and Joanne has never revealed the details of these early works.

⋜ A VISION ON A TRAIN ⋜

In 1990, twenty-five-year-old Joanne and her boyfriend from
the University of Exeter decided to move to Manchester. On
a train journey after a weekend of failed apartment hunting,
a flash of inspiration came that would change her life.
On the way to London, the train broke down. Joanne was
gazing out the window at cows in a field when suddenly,
as she describes it, "the idea for Harry Potter simply fell
into my head." She had no idea what had prompted it, but
in that moment she pictured a boy who does not know
he has magic powers receiving an invitation to attend
wizard school. It was the most stimulating story idea
she had ever had. Unusually, Joanne didn't have a pen
or notebook with her, so she spent a few hours sitting
quietly and dreaming up Harry's story. Several other
characters popped into her head, too:
Ron Weasley, Hagrid, and
the irritating ghosts Nearly
Headless Nick and Peeves.
The outline of Hogwarts
came to her as well.

Railroads were significant in Joanne's life. Her parents had met on that train traveling from King's Cross to Scotland, and now she'd dreamed up Harry Potter on a train journey. Perhaps those events explain why the Hogwarts Express became such an important element in her stories.

Joanne and her boyfriend finally found an apartment in Manchester and settled down. Once again, Joanne began to take on various secretarial jobs. She worked at the Manchester Chamber of Commerce and was employed at the University of Manchester for a while.

Although she was quite bored at work, Joanne now had a secret hobby to feed her active mind. In her spare time, she began to shape Harry Potter's world, keeping her handwritten notes in a shoebox. Harry became so much a part of her life that she would daydream about the wizarding world while she was supposed to be taking notes in meetings. Joanne had decided that there would be seven books, one for every year of Harry's education at Hogwarts.

The basic idea of the Harry Potter story was clear already: Harry grows up in the Muggle world before discovering he is a wizard. When he turns eleven, he goes to Hogwarts to train in wizarding skills: making potions, casting spells, flying on a broomstick, and caring for magical creatures. And he begins to fulfill his special role in the struggle between good and evil in the magical world.

Childhood Memories

Joanne feels strongly that only people who can remember what it is like to be a child should write children's books. She says she is able to travel back to her childhood in her mind and see the world as she did then. To write characters well, an author needs to be able to understand what they might be thinking, so Joanne's ability was useful. She could imagine what it would be like to be Harry and his friends in every year at Hogwarts.

I remember vividly what it felt like to be eleven and every age up to twenty.

⋛ SAD TIMES ⋜

When Joanne went home to her parents for Christmas in December 1990, she didn't know that it would be the last time she would see her mother alive. Although Anne was only forty-five, she had become severely disabled with MS. Joanne returned to Manchester after the family's holiday gathering. On New Year's Eve, her father called at 7:30 a.m. to tell her the awful news that her beloved mother had died the night before.

   Anne's death had a huge effect on Jo. Torn up by grief, she could not concentrate on her work. She also realized she was fed up with her relationship and felt she needed a major life change. Following a horrible argument, Joanne split up with her boyfriend, stormed out of their home, and booked herself into a hotel in Didsbury, in the Manchester suburbs. That evening, sitting quietly with her thoughts after the drama, she dreamed up the game of Quidditch.

Quidditch: The Wizarding Sport

A fast, energetic game, Quidditch is played high in the air on broomsticks in an oval Quidditch stadium.

→ Two teams compete for points, scored by throwing the 12-inch (30.1 cm) Quaffle (ball) through one of three hoops at the end of the pitch (field).

→ Each team has seven players: a Keeper (goal keeper), a Seeker, three Chasers (goal scorers), and two Beaters.

→ There are two balls called Bludgers. The Beaters swing bats to fire Bludgers at their opponents while protecting their own team members from incoming Bludgers.

→ The Seeker tries to find and catch the tiny, enchanted Golden Snitch, which wins the team 150 points and usually means they win the match.

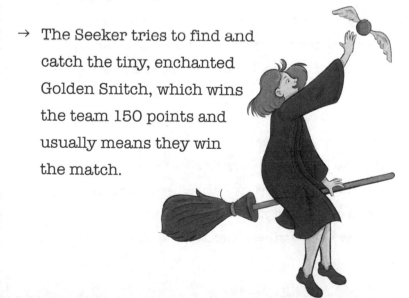

⋛ NEW COUNTRY, NEW LIFE ⋛

Now Joanne had to figure out what to do next. In 1991, a few months after her mother died, she spotted an advertisement for English teachers to work at the Encounter English School in Porto, Portugal, teaching English to adults at all levels, from beginners up. It was not necessary to have a teaching qualification to offer English classes abroad; a degree from a British university was enough. Joanne was looking for a complete change—and this opportunity seemed ideal.

Joanne bravely set off alone, ready to start a new life. The situation turned out to be perfect. She shared an apartment with two other teachers who were also in their mid-twenties—Aine Kiely from Ireland and Jill Prewett from England. The trio became firm friends. It was a relaxed lifestyle: Joanne taught her classes from 5 to 10 p.m., so she had much of the day free for writing. She was busily working on her Harry Potter book, writing away for hours in coffee shops around the city. Joanne was also practicing her drawing and became quite skilled at pen-and-ink sketches. She often liked to sketch her characters and draw scenes from the book.

The Porto Cloaks

A city and port in northern Portugal, Porto is the country's second-largest city and is known for its strong, sweet port wine. Interestingly, Porto's university uniform is a suit and tie, covered by a black cloak to protect the wearer from rain. The uniform is not required, but some students like to wear it. Over the winter months, Joanne would have seen students wandering through Porto in their cloaks. Maybe the outfit gave her the idea for the cloaks of Hogwarts.

⋝ TIME TO WRITE ⋜

Because she had recently experienced the loss of her mother, Joanne was able to write movingly about Harry's feelings about the loss of his parents. While in Portugal, she wrote a poignant chapter in the first book, "The Mirror of Erised" (Erised is *desire* spelled backward). People see what they desire most in the mirror. Harry desperately misses his parents, and he sees them waving at him, along with members of the Potter family he's never met. Maybe Joanne imagined herself looking in the mirror and seeing Anne smiling out at her.

Joanne treasured the time and space to sit alone and write, but she also wanted to get to know some Portuguese people. She became friendly with Maria Inês Aguiar, the assistant director of the language school where she worked. Maria helped Joanne learn Portuguese, although she never became fluent—she found it difficult to practice the local language because she spoke English to her students and lived with her English-speaking friends. Jo, Aine, and Jill used to go to a club called Swing on Saturday nights, where DJs played English hits, and the group would chat, laugh, and dance.

A NEW ROMANCE

One evening when Joanne was out with her friends in a bar called Meia Cava, she met Jorge Arantes. Joanne was open to meeting new people and was happy to start talking to him. Jorge spoke English, and the pair talked for a couple of hours. At the end of the evening, they swapped phone numbers and agreed to meet again.

A few years younger than Joanne, Jorge was a journalism student. Like Joanne, he loved reading, and soon they were spending lots of time together. Jorge used to meet Joanne in a café near her language school, and they would drink coffee and discuss books. The couple began to live together in Jorge's mother's apartment, with Joanne paying for their food and other expenses from her earnings. Joanne revealed to Jorge that she was working on a novel, introducing him to her private world of Harry Potter. Years later, Jorge claimed he had made suggestions for the book, but Joanne insists that statement is untrue. Even back then, Joanne dreamed of her book being sold in bookshops. She didn't know that her dream would come true—several million times over!

> "[Jorge] had as much input into Harry Potter as I had in *A Tale of Two Cities* [by Charles Dickens]."
> —J. K. Rowling

≡ HOW JOANNE WRITES ≡

During her time in Portugal, Joanne developed her writing method. Like most authors, she spends a long time planning her work before she puts pen to paper, deciding the plot for the entire story. She enjoys thinking up interesting and amusing names for all the creatures, people, and places. Joanne develops each character, creating their entire back story—their life before they come into the book. That way, she really understands the characters and why they act as they do. She keeps notes on all of the characters' actions in case she needs to refer to them in future books.

For example, Ron has a rat called Scabbers. He's an elderly, hand-me-down rat that has been in the Weasley family for years. Ron thinks he is mostly useless. But Scabbers is not exactly as he seems. And all of Scabbers's actions in the stories—until his true nature is revealed—fit with the character Joanne developed for him.

Although Joanne plans her characters extremely carefully, she does not settle every detail of the story but works out some developments as she is writing. She finds it is more fun to come up with a few surprises along the way. Joanne always writes her stories by hand and then types them up. After, she edits her writing to check that the story line works and that it fits with what has happened before. She makes sure to include humor, so there are light touches even when the story is sad or scary. Joanne says that she wrote fifteen versions of chapter one of *Harry Potter and the Philosopher's Stone*. That might sound incredible, but authors often rewrite every chapter many times before a book is finished.

Philosopher vs. Sorcerer

J. K. Rowling's first book would come out in the United States as *Harry Potter and the Sorcerer's Stone*. The US publisher did not believe readers would be familiar with the word *philosopher*.

⋛ LOVE AND LOSS ⋜

Back in the non-magical world, in August 1992,
Jorge proposed to Joanne, and the couple married on
October 16, 1992. Their daughter, Jessica, was born in
July 1993—Joanne says she named their little girl after
Jessica Mitford. She adored her baby and adapted easily
and happily to being a mom. Life seemed to be turning
out well for Joanne. Living in a beautiful city and good at
her job, she was now mother to a wonderful baby.

Although Jorge and Joanne loved each other, they
soon began to grow apart. Jorge had done his national
service in the army but had not yet found a job—it had
always been Joanne who paid for everything, which
seemed unfair. Joanne and Jorge argued a lot.

In November 1993, during a particularly nasty
argument, Joanne told Jorge she did not love him
anymore. In a rage, he dragged her into the street,
throwing her out of their home as their four-month-old
baby slept indoors. Joanne ran to Aine and Jill for help,
and they contacted Maria from the language school.
Along with a police-officer friend, Maria turned up at
Jorge's home in the morning to demand that he hand
over Jessica—which he did.

Once reunited with her daughter, Joanne made up
her mind to leave Jorge and Portugal for good. For a
couple of weeks, she and Jessica went into hiding with
friends Jorge did not know. Joanne arranged for their
speedy departure while Jorge tried in vain to track
them down. The couple's life together had lasted only
thirteen months.

Joanne knew she wanted to go back to the United
Kingdom. But she had no idea what to do and how
she would manage alone, with no job, no home, and
a young baby.

Milestones of Life

Several significant dates from real life found their way into Jo's writing. For example, she shares her birthday with her hero—July 31—and it is on Harry's 11th birthday that he discovers he is a wizard. And in *Harry Potter and the Prisoner of Azkaban*, Professor Trelawney, a divination teacher who claims to be able to see into the future, tells student Lavender Brown that the thing Lavender is dreading will happen on October 16—Joanne's wedding day to Jorge.

CHAPTER 4

THE PATH TO PUBLICATION

In December 1993, Joanne moved to Edinburgh, Scotland, to be close to her sister, Di. It was hard for her to find a job because she could not afford childcare for a small baby. She had little choice but to register as unemployed, which involved filling out lots of forms and explaining her stressful escape from Portugal.

Joanne was able to claim welfare benefits, but they were not generous, and the hardship she would face soon hit her: "I realized I was about to start living on £70 [$105] a week." That amount had to cover bills, food, and everything else for her and her baby. That Christmas, she found herself playing the band REM's song "Everybody Hurts" over and over again. It suited her miserable mood perfectly.

Joanne and Jessica lived in a small one-bedroom apartment. It was cold and dark, and there were unwelcome guests. "If I concentrated hard enough, I'd be able to block out the sounds of mice behind the [baseboard]," Joanne recalled.

Joanne resolved to improve her difficult situation. That winter, she borrowed £600 ($900) from her good friend Sean Harris so she could afford the deposit on a better apartment. It was almost impossible to find a real-estate agent who would rent a home to someone with very little money. Eventually, she found a one-bedroom, unfurnished apartment in Leith, an up-and-coming part of Edinburgh with new shops and cafés emerging. Jo's friends and Di were able to lend Joanne some furniture so she could move in. This was a step up.

Life was still tough, though. Joanne found it embarrassing to collect her benefit check in town. She thought that people saw her as a person with no value because she could not work for a living, and she felt humiliated by being poor. One nurse tried to be kind by giving some old toys to Jessica, but it made Joanne feel upset that she couldn't afford to buy these things for her daughter, and so she threw away the gifts.

"Poverty is not an ennobling experience. Poverty entails fear, and stress, and sometimes depression; it means a thousand petty humiliations and hardships." —J. K. Rowling

⋛ THE DEPTHS OF DEPRESSION ⋚

To add to her troubles, Jorge arrived from Portugal in March 1994 to try to find Joanne and their daughter. Joanne was alarmed—she was frightened of Jorge and had no intention of meeting him. She was forced to go to lawyers to get a restraining order to stop him from coming near her or Jessica. A few months later, she applied for a divorce.

Joanne was depressed at this point. So much had happened in the past three years, and deep feelings about the loss of her mother came to the surface again. Apart from spending time with her daughter, the main activity that helped Joanne survive this painful time was writing. Many characters were influenced by her own experiences. Both Harry and Hermione are like Joanne in some ways: Harry has endured terrible loss, and Hermione is clever and hardworking but insecure. As Joanne has explained, "Hermione . . . is based almost entirely on myself at the age of eleven. . . . Like Hermione, I was obsessed with achieving academically, but this masked a huge insecurity." Ron is a loyal friend, rather like Jo's companion Sean Harris.

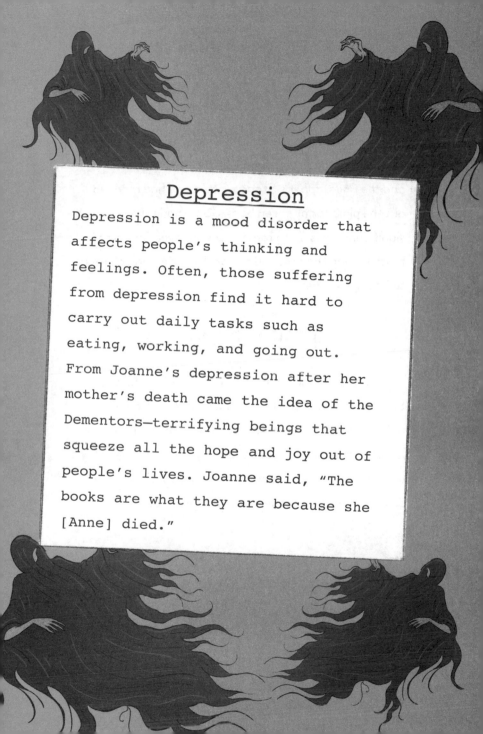

Depression

Depression is a mood disorder that affects people's thinking and feelings. Often, those suffering from depression find it hard to carry out daily tasks such as eating, working, and going out. From Joanne's depression after her mother's death came the idea of the Dementors—terrifying beings that squeeze all the hope and joy out of people's lives. Joanne said, "The books are what they are because she [Anne] died."

Joanne managed to emerge from depression slowly, with counseling sessions to help her.

On her return to the United Kingdom, Joanne already had the first three chapters of *Harry Potter and the Philosopher's Stone* written and had mapped out the plots for all seven books. She made the significant decision to remain unemployed for a year, finish writing the first volume of the series, and attempt to find a publisher.

⋛ COFFEE AND WIZARDS ⋚

Joanne was still unsure about her writing abilities. She shyly showed the first three chapters of the book to her sister, who really enjoyed them. Di laughed out loud, because she thought the story was so funny and well written. This gave Joanne the confidence to believe that other readers would enjoy it, too.

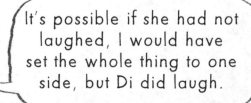

It's possible if she had not laughed, I would have set the whole thing to one side, but Di did laugh.

Joanne had always liked writing in cafés, and the story of her creating Harry Potter in a coffee shop has become well known. She used to leave her little apartment every morning with Jessica in her stroller. When Jessica fell asleep, Joanne went to sit in Nicolson's Café, a restaurant owned by Di's husband, Roger, and his friend Dougal McBride. The staff became used to Joanne sitting there, nursing one cup of coffee and writing for a couple of hours.

It was good for Joanne to be outside in the world. Although it was stressful being short of money, she had a few close friends and her sister to support her, and immersing herself in Harry's world helped greatly. A friend looked after Jessica for a couple of hours once a week so Joanne could have a complete break.

⌇ TRAINING TO TEACH ⌇

Joanne never expected to make a living from writing books, so she had to find a job. In late 1994, she chose to take on a couple of hours of secretarial work each week to earn a little extra money for food, toys, and clothes for Jessica. But she realized as well that she should try to develop a career.

Joanne opted to train as a schoolteacher, thinking that her experience at Porto's language school would be helpful. She needed to take a one-year Post-Graduate Certificate in Education (PGCE) course to qualify, and she applied to do a PGCE in modern languages. Competition for admission was tough; only a quarter of applicants were accepted.

Fortunately, Joanne's application was successful, and she was invited to start her course in August 1995.

Joanne was relieved—this would be her path out of poverty. The only hitch was paying for childcare. Luckily, a kind friend loaned her some money in the summer of 1995. Joanne was worried that she would never be able to repay the loan—but that turned out not to be a problem. . . .

Things are looking up!

Joanne became a full-time student. She received a grant—a sum of money that covers living expenses—so she did not have to work. To her immense relief, she no longer needed welfare benefits; there would be no more unpleasant weekly trips to pick up a check at the post office. Her divorce had come through in June, so she could finally begin to move on.

Joanne embarked on her training to teach in high school. It took her a while to adjust, but within a few months, she was doing extremely well. Imaginative and creative, she invented a card game for language practice, drawing the cards herself. She used magazines, crosswords, diagrams, and pictures to make her lessons enjoyable for the students. Notably, she created a happy atmosphere in class. Joanne felt strongly that teachers should be encouraging and never bully the children. She received high grades for her teaching practice and graduated in the summer of 1996.

⋝ PUBLISHING POTTER ⋜

Joanne now expected to make a living as a teacher, but she hadn't forgotten about Harry Potter. She finished writing the first book in late 1995, after five long years, and was determined that the world would meet her boy wizard.

Joanne had typed all 90,000 words of *Harry Potter and the Philosopher's Stone* on a typewriter. Rather than pay to have the pages photocopied, she typed the whole book again so that she could keep a copy.

<u>How to Get Published</u>

For new authors, many hurdles stand in the way of getting their first novel in print. Once they have completed their manuscript, fiction writers usually need to find a literary agent, a person who advises authors on how to improve their work and search for a publisher. Agents accept books they believe are well written and on a topic that will appeal to publishers. The agent usually asks the author to rewrite parts of the book. Then the agent sends the manuscript to different publishing companies. Writers often experience rejection after rejection and may never have their book accepted. Nowadays, some writers publish their books themselves—but they have to pay all the costs.

Now Joanne needed to find a literary agent. At the start of 1996, she looked up agents in the *Writers' and Artists' Yearbook*—a resource guide for writers—in Edinburgh Library. The first one she contacted turned her down. The second was Christopher Little.

It was the best letter of my life. I read it eight times.

Bryony Evans was an English literature graduate working as an assistant at the Christopher Little Literary Agency in London. Just like Jo, the twenty-five-year-old Bryony loved fantasy books. The agency did not generally deal with children's titles, so Joanne's manuscript had been chucked into the rejection basket, ready to be returned to the author. Bryony happened to be checking the basket when she noticed an unusual black plastic folder and was intrigued. Inside were three sample chapters with Jo's illustrations. Bryony started reading Harry's story and could not put it down—she was hooked. Convinced it was worth publishing, she handed it to Fleur Howle, a reader who evaluated new submissions for the agency. Fleur was greatly impressed, too, and the pair persuaded Christopher to take on this unknown author.

Bryony asked Joanne to send the entire book, and both she and Christopher sped through it. There was little they thought Joanne should change, although Christopher thought the game of Quidditch should be more central to the plot. Joanne sent him her hand-drawn picture of a match and the rules, and the deal was sealed. The new author received a standard contract to stay with the agency for five years.

WHO WILL PUBLISH HARRY POTTER?

Harry Potter and the Philosopher's Stone was now in Christopher Little's hands, and the agency hunted for a publisher. Although Christopher was sure it was a winner, Joanne's book was rejected by twelve companies. Finally, in August 1996, Bloomsbury Publishing agreed to publish it. Barry Cunningham was head of children's books. He found the book "terribly exciting. What struck me first was that the book came with a fully imagined world. . . . It was, however, very long for a children's book at that time." Bloomsbury offered Joanne an advance payment of £1,500 ($2,300) and said her book would be launched in June 1997. Absolutely thrilled, Joanne traveled all the way from Edinburgh to London and back in a day to have lunch with Barry.

You'll never make any money out of children's books, Jo.

Reassured by the contract for the first title, Joanne was now writing the next book in the series. In autumn 1996, she started working as a substitute teacher. She was still low on funds because she had no regular teaching work and had childcare costs. Joanne applied for a bursary (a gift of money) from the Scottish Arts Council to help her complete her book. Joanne was awarded the highest amount possible: £8,000 ($12,500)—a fortune for a new writer. She used some of it to buy her first computer. The grant showed that the Arts Council believed in her abilities.

What's in a Name?

The editors at Bloomsbury were worried that a female author's name might put off boy readers. Joanne adopted *K* as a middle initial—from her beloved grandmother Kathleen—and J. K. Rowling was born. As long as the book was published, the name didn't matter to her.

⋛ POTTER IN PRINT ⋚

In June 1997, *Harry Potter and the Philosopher's Stone* was published, introducing the first part of Harry's story to the public. When eleven-year-old Harry receives a visitor from Hogwarts School of Witchcraft and Wizardry, he is shocked to hear he's a wizard. He also learns that his parents were murdered by an evil wizard who was not able to kill Harry—for that reason, Harry is a celebrity in the magical world. Having been brought up in the Muggle world, this is all news to Harry. He starts at Hogwarts, makes friends for the first time ever, finds out he is a natural at Quidditch, and becomes fascinated with this strange wizarding world..

But no grand celebrations greeted the arrival of Harry Potter in bookstores. Since Joanne was a new author, Bloomsbury did not arrange a big book launch, and they printed only five hundred hardcover copies. Nevertheless, Joanne was incredibly proud. She told Barry it was like "having a baby all over again." It had taken her seven years from having the idea to holding the book in her hand. On the date of publication, she carried a copy around with her all day and loved finding it in bookshops. It was a magical experience.

A first-edition hardcover copy of *Harry Potter and the Philosopher's Stone* in fine condition now sells for £75,000 ($95,000). Check your bookshelves, closets, and attics!

CHAPTER 5

A STUNNING SUCCESS

Joanne was happy to read a couple of encouraging reviews of *Harry Potter and the Philosopher's Stone* in the Scottish newspaper *The Scotsman* and the English *Sunday Times*. These reviews would certainly help sell the book.

28 June 1997

THE SCOTSMAN

Harry Potter Book Review

"If you buy or borrow nothing else this summer for the young readers in your family, you must get hold of a copy of *Harry Potter and the Philosopher's Stone*. . . .

What distinguishes this novel from so many other fantasies is its grip on reality. Harry is a hugely likeable child . . . competitive but always compassionate. . . . [J. K. Rowling] is a first-rate writer for children."

⋛ REACHING AMERICAN READERS ⋛

Then, within just three days of publication, an extraordinary thing occurred. Not only was Joanne's book published in the United Kingdom, but US publishers were suddenly fighting over the right to bring out Harry Potter. It was fantastic news for the British author to discover that her book would be published in the United States, where there are millions more readers. The winner of the battle was Arthur Levine of Scholastic, who had eagerly read the book from cover to cover during a flight to Italy. Arthur loved it so much that he was prepared to risk paying the enormous sum of $100,000 (around £60,000) to Joanne to publish her work in the United States, the world's largest market for children's books. It was an unheard-of amount to offer for a children's title from an unknown author.

The news of the American deal was a complete shock to Joanne, who said, "I walked around the flat for hours in a kind of nervous frenzy." The deal created lots of hype. For the press, Joanne presented a perfect rags-to-riches story, and all the major newspapers wanted to interview her. Joanne did not enjoy being the center of attention, but the positive publicity definitely helped spread the word about Harry Potter, and sales of the book rocketed.

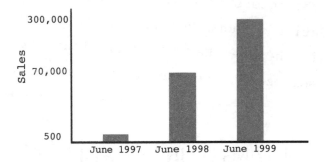

THE CHAMBER OF SECRETS

Just a couple of weeks after the first Harry Potter book came out, Joanne delivered the manuscript for the next volume, *Harry Potter and the Chamber of Secrets*. In this title, Harry's friend Ron Weasley and Ron's mischievous older brothers help Harry escape in a flying Ford Anglia. In the book, Joanne addresses the problem of wizards' prejudice against Muggles. Some pure-blooded wizards, born into magical families, look down on people whose parents are Muggles. But Harry and his friends strongly oppose this view. They believe that wizards and witches are equal and that there's nothing wrong with being a Muggle.

Some critics felt that Joanne could have included more racially and ethnically diverse characters in the books. There are a few characters of color, such as the twins Parvati and Padma Patil, and Cho Chang—who briefly becomes Harry's girlfriend later in the series—but they do not play major roles.

⤙ MOVING UP IN THE WORLD ⤚

In the first year alone, 70,000 copies of *Harry Potter and the Philosopher's Stone* were sold—a phenomenal success for a first-time author. Joanne was able to give up teaching and become a full-time writer. But she was determined to put Jessica first and always be there for her daughter.

The deal with Scholastic meant Joanne could afford to leave her rented apartment in Leith and buy a house. In the summer of 1998, she and her daughter moved to Hazelbank Terrace in a suburb of Edinburgh. It was a street occupied by lots of ordinary families with young children. Here, Jessica could have her own bedroom for the first time and would have plenty of friends.

In September, Jessica started at nearby Craiglockhart Primary School, along with the other children on the street. At first, the other parents had no idea that they had a bestselling author in their midst. Joanne tried to keep it secret to protect her daughter's privacy. After dropping off Jessica at school, Joanne headed to work—usually to a café to write her third Harry Potter book. She had to switch to different cafés to get some peace and quiet, since Nicolson's Café had become a stop on the Harry Potter tourist trail, with fans gathering to see if they could spot her.

The schoolchildren at Craiglockhart School eventually found out who Joanne was, and she agreed to do a book reading for them. She also started reading the stories to Jessica, who was curious to know what all the fuss was about.

Luckily, Jessica was young when her mother became

well known, so it all seemed normal to her. She was not particularly excited when Joanne revealed one day that she was about to speak on the radio. Jessica could hear her mother talking any day of the week, so why would she bother to tune in?

PRIZEWINNER

As the Harry Potter books were so highly praised, author prizes started flooding in. Joanne won her first prize in 1997, the Nestlé Smarties Book Prize Gold Medal (9–11 years), for *Harry Potter and the Philosopher's Stone*. It was rapidly followed by many more, including the highly respected "Nibby," the British Book Award for Children's Book of the Year, in 1997.

Harry Potter soon became an international success, too. After it hit bookstores in the United States, publishers around the world rushed to buy the rights to sell it in their countries.

Interestingly, the Harry Potter books appealed to adults as well as children. It was unusual for children's titles to be read so widely by adults. Perhaps the length of the books helped—they were far longer than most children's novels, and adult readers got into the stories.

⋛ ROLLING OUT THE SERIES ⋛

Teachers and librarians were delighted by the growing popularity of Harry Potter. In the playground and classroom, children were discussing the magical world of Hogwarts and encouraging others to read the books. Teachers noticed that children were reading more in general. The second book, *Harry Potter and the Chamber of Secrets,* shot to the top of the bestseller list as soon as it was released. Joanne's publishers were overjoyed and offered her a contract to write the rest of the seven books. Of course, she had already planned them out, but now she had to complete them to regular deadlines to feed the appetites of her readers.

Joanne had worked out how her tale would finish when she'd first devised the plot. She wrote the final chapter and kept it locked in a hidden safe so that the end of the story would remain secret until the publication of the final title.

TITLE	UK	US
Philosopher's Stone (*Sorcerer's Stone* in the US)	June 1997	Jan. 1998
Chamber of Secrets	July 1998	Feb. 1999
Prisoner of Azkaban	July 1999	August 1999
Goblet of Fire	July 2000	July 2000
Order of the Phoenix	June 2003	June 2003
Half-Blood Prince	July 2005	July 2005
Deathly Hallows	July 2007	July 2007

THE PRISONER OF AZKABAN

In July 1999, *Harry Potter and the Prisoner of Azkaban* came out. In this tale, Harry finds out more about how his parents died and who was responsible. He also comes face to face with the Dementors, who suck all the happiness out of people.

Joanne says you have to be careful what you invent, especially when you are writing a long series in which actions in an early volume can affect what happens later. In this title, she introduced "time-turners"— devices that allow wizards and witches to travel back in time. Hogwarts headmaster Albus Dumbledore gives Hermione special permission to use one so that she can study two classes at the same time and squeeze even more lessons into her busy schedule. After her first 9 a.m. class, she goes back in time by one hour to take the second one. But it dawned on Joanne that if wizards could go back in time, they could solve problems in the past, and her plots would not work. She adjusted the story line of the future novels to make sure that all the time-turners would be destroyed, so wizards would no longer have this option.

I love writing these books. I don't think anyone could enjoy reading them more than I enjoy writing them.

⋛ RICHES AND CELEBRITY ⋛

By June 1999, Joanne's personal life had changed completely since her days of poverty in a tiny apartment in Edinburgh. As an author, Joanne received royalties: a small part of the price customers pay for each book. Her growing wealth provided her with a comfortable life, and she was on the verge of becoming a millionaire. Along with riches came celebrity status.

Achieving success, wealth, and fame may seem wonderful, but it can also be a challenge. The media were fascinated by Joanne. She received so many invitations to give interviews and talks and to attend book signings that she barely had time to write. Every day, hundreds of letters from fans reached her mailbox.

As a naturally shy person, she found the attention quite overwhelming. She rarely went to writers' gatherings, preferring not to mix regularly with other authors. The residents of Hazelbank Terrace knew she was famous but did not interfere. They allowed Joanne to try to maintain her family's privacy so that her daughter could enjoy a normal life.

Nothing prepared Joanne for the reaction she received in the United States, though. In October 1999, she went on a book tour across the country with *Harry Potter and the Prisoner of Azkaban*. It was this book that turned Joanne into a celebrity in America. When she arrived at Politics and Prose bookstore in Washington, DC, the line was so long, she thought the shop was holding a massive sale. As she drew closer, she saw a sea of wands and witches' hats—hundreds and hundreds of children were waiting excitedly to meet her. Joanne was pleased to see them; she has always been comfortable and relaxed talking to her young readers. She signed 1,400 books before being whisked off to the next event to repeat the performance. By now, her Harry Potter titles filled the top three places on the *New York Times* bestseller list.

Book signing with
J. K. Rowling
TODAY

HARRY POTTER'S REAL-LIFE ENEMIES

Not everyone loved Harry Potter. Some Christians, especially in the United States—where more than half of the books are sold—opposed the books for religious reasons. They thought the books created an unhealthy interest in witchcraft and showed it as a positive force, which was against their Christian values. In South Carolina, some parents complained to the state's board of education. One mother believed the book contained "a serious tone of death, hate, lack of respect, and sheer evil." Some people tried to get the book banned. Yet others disagreed with this approach. The American Library Association has stated that parents should figure out for themselves which books are suitable for their own children.

UNFAIR TO GIRLS?

Some feminists felt that girls are not always shown in a positive way, because Harry is the hero and often uses his strength to rescue Hermione. It's always female characters, such as Molly Weasley, who cook delicious meals for their families—apparently, even witches cannot conjure food out of thin air. And at upsetting moments, Hermione bursts into floods of tears, but Harry does not cry. Feminist academic Elizabeth Heilman thought J. K. Rowling portrayed girls as "giggly, emotional, gossipy, and anti-intellectual." Joanne denied this, explaining that Hermione is highly intelligent and logical and has a strong sense of right and wrong. Hermione's skills are different from Harry's but equally significant.

⋛ SECRETS REVEALED ⋚

Joanne came under fire from the media, too. Reporters from newspapers all around the world dug hard to unearth stories about her private life, hoping to persuade people to buy their papers. In November 1999, journalists uncovered Joanne's marriage to Jorge Arantes. The British newspaper *Daily Express* paid Jorge thousands of dollars to tell his side of the story, and a version also appeared in the *Mail on Sunday*. Jorge's outpouring was particularly upsetting for Joanne because Jorge claimed that he had helped write Harry Potter. Joanne has stated that there is no truth to the claim whatsoever.

For a while, the nasty revelations about her relationship with Jorge affected Joanne and took her attention away from her writing. In the Harry Potter books, she created the vile *Daily Prophet* journalist Rita Skeeter, perhaps inspired by her own experiences with the press. Rita enters the scene in the fourth book, when Harry is truly famous. An Animagus, Rita is able to switch from human to beetle form and spy on people easily. She makes up stories about people and publishes them as fact. Rita mistreats Harry in much the same way Joanne feels she was badly treated by the media.

"I HELPED WRITE HARRY POTTER . . ."

Joanne realized how careful she needed to be about her contact with the media and became increasingly cautious about giving interviews. Her privacy would become even more crucial as Hollywood studios started to tussle over who would bring Harry Potter to the big screen—and bring even more fame and fortune to his creator.

CHAPTER 6

HARRY ON THE BIG SCREEN

With all the buzz about the books, it was only a
matter of time before the movie studios caught
on. They knew Harry Potter's adventures would
make excellent films. Yet Joanne wanted her say.
She would allow movies to be made only if she
could approve the director, the screenplay (the
script written for the film), and the merchandise
ideas. Joanne insisted that the films be produced
in the United Kingdom with British actors. It was
exceptional for a writer to be given so much power
over the making of movies.

In 1999, Warner Bros. won the rights to make the
films. The plan was to make one movie per book (in
the end, eight were made). Director Chris Columbus
was signed up in March 2000. Chris's daughter was
a huge Harry Potter fan, so he was already familiar
with the wizarding world. He went to meet Joanne,
and she said she was happy with the choice of
director—the pair would be working closely together.

⋛ THE HARRY POTTER HEROES ⋛

Next came the tricky task of casting three young actors
to play Harry, Hermione, and Ron. Daniel Radcliffe was
selected to play Harry. At age eleven, Daniel already
had acting experience, and he was to be paid £200,000
($300,000) for the first two movies. That's a lot of
pocket money for an eleven-year-old! Rupert Grint,
also eleven, was cast as Ron, while Emma Watson, in the
role of Hermione, was just ten. When Joanne met the
actors, she was confident they suited their parts.

    The movie studio was taking a considerable risk,
though. Not only were two of their stars unknown child
actors, but they would also have to start filming the
second movie before they knew if the first one was
successful.

Daniel, Rupert, and Emma spent most of their teenage years acting in the Harry Potter films. Children have to continue their schoolwork while filming, so a tutor was hired to travel with them. They studied for five hours every day—not much less than students at regular schools.

⋛ A STAR-STUDDED CAST ⋚

Joanne had always hoped that the Scottish comic actor Robbie Coltrane would play the half-giant Hagrid, and she was delighted when he agreed. The remaining costars were all well-loved British actors.

CAST

Professor McGonagall	**DAME MAGGIE SMITH**
Severus Snape	**ALAN RICKMAN**
Albus Dumbledore	**RICHARD HARRIS**
Molly Weasley	**DAME JULIE WALTERS**
Nearly Headless Nick	**JOHN CLEESE**
Bellatrix Lestrange	**HELENA BONHAM-CARTER**

Joanne was deeply involved with the movies. She frequently visited the set, and at night she watched the rushes—the unedited scenes filmed that day.

EXTRAORDINARY EFFECTS

The Creature Shop, a special-effects company, made the magical creatures. For *Harry Potter and the Prisoner of Azkaban,* the company made three versions of Buckbeak the Hippogriff: one standing, one rearing up, and one lying down. The models were based on birds, particularly the golden eagle, and the creators consulted vets to make sure the proportions of Buckbeak were correct. It was painstaking work—the team had to glue on each feather individually.

Talented artists created a model of Hogwarts School in miniature so that a green screen could be used to film impressive outside scenes. When the cameras filmed Harry Potter flying around on his broomstick, he "flew" against a green background. Later, the green background was removed digitally and replaced with the dramatic landscape around Hogwarts Castle.

The production team scoured the United Kingdom for good locations for filming. Parts of Gloucester Cathedral and other cathedrals and abbeys were deemed perfect for scenes inside Hogwarts Castle. The Australian High Commission in London was chosen for the imposing goblin-run Gringotts Bank. The team also selected Leadenhall Market in London—a beautiful market built in 1881—for the outside of Diagon Alley.

⋛ "POTTER FOUR" ⋚

Although Joanne was becoming increasingly famous, she still needed to keep up her writing routine to complete the rest of the series. During 1999, she was working on the fourth book. It caused her some difficulties, and she had to make several significant changes to the plot. In this title, fourteen-year-old Harry is entered into the Triwizard Tournament against wizards from different countries—even though the minimum age for entry has always been seventeen. He has to undergo dangerous missions, including seizing a golden egg from a dragon and spending an hour underwater to rescue Ron from the bottom of a lake. During the course of the book, Voldemort finally gathers enough strength to take human form once again and confront Harry in person in a dramatic battle.

This volume was far longer than previous titles—636 pages—and much thicker than almost any other children's book on the market. But fans were as eager to read it as ever. To build up suspense, the name of the book was not released before publication. In the book world, it was simply called "Potter Four."

$\succeq$ POTTERMANIA $\preceq$

Bloomsbury decided that for the first time, the new installment of Harry's adventures would be published on the same date in July 2000 in the United Kingdom and the United States. It was revealed that a death would occur in "Potter Four," leading to an explosion of Pottermania. Fans held heated discussions about who it could possibly be, and whether they would have to say goodbye to a favorite character.

Bloomsbury planned to launch the title—finally revealed as *Harry Potter and the Goblet of Fire*—at King's Cross station in London. They mocked up Platform 9¾, and hundreds of fans, journalists, and photographers turned up, hoping to meet J. K. Rowling. It was pandemonium. The platform area was so crowded that it was impossible for Joanne to get off the special old-fashioned train she had arrived on to meet her fans. The train quickly departed, with Joanne calling "sorry" to all the disappointed children.

PLATFORM 9 3/4

Platform 9¾

In Harry Potter's world, enthusiastic young wizards and witches gather at King's Cross station on September 1 each year. Appearing as a brick wall to Muggles, Platform 9¾ is the secret gateway to board the scarlet Hogwarts Express. In honor of J. K. Rowling's books, in 2012, a sign was erected at King's Cross station to mark the phantom platform, with a half-disappeared luggage trolley beneath it. A Harry Potter gift shop opened next to it. Platform 9¾ soon became a crowded tourist spot, with fans from around the world lining up to have photos taken by a professional photographer as they pushed the trolley against the wall.

⋛ HONORS AND AWARDS ⋚

Within three years, J. K. Rowling had become a household name worldwide. In 2000, the University of Exeter awarded her an honorary degree, a special honor reserved for only the most outstanding former students. Professor Peter Wiseman introduced Joanne and described how her success could be credited to three key ingredients. First, she had natural talent and practiced writing stories over many years. Second, Joanne went through tough times, but she overcame them, which strengthened her character and made her determined to succeed. Third, she worked incredibly hard to achieve her goal of becoming an author.

In her acceptance speech, Joanne talked about her failures—being miserable in Manchester, hating office work, and attempting to write adult books. She said she had found the courage to finish the first Harry Potter adventure when she had nothing to lose—her marriage had broken down, and she had no job and no money.

Prizes for Harry Potter

Joanne seemed extremely modest when accepting her honorary degree. Yet it was just one award of many—she has received a remarkable number of prizes for the Harry Potter books. Here are some of the early awards; Joanne has won many more since.

→ 1997 Nestlé Smarties Book Prize Gold Medal (9–11 years) for *The Philosopher's Stone*

→ 1998 British Book Awards (nicknamed the "Nibbies" and similar to the Oscars in the movie industry) Children's Book of the Year for *The Chamber of Secrets*

→ 1999 Whitbread Children's Book of the Year Award for *The Prisoner of Azkaban*

→ 2000 British Book Awards Author of the Year

→ 2001 Order of the British Empire (OBE)—a special royal honor from the queen, for services to children's literature

⇃ ABSENT AT THE AWARDS ⇂

On January 25, 2000, the actor Stephen Fry collected
Joanne's prize for the Whitbread Children's Book of the
Year on her behalf because she was ill with the flu. They
had become friends when he recorded the audiobook
versions of her books. Joanne was also unable to
collect her OBE from the queen in person because it
clashed with Jessica's school Nativity play. She wrote
a polite note explaining that her daughter was unwell
as an excuse. Prince Charles invited the author to the
royal castle at Balmoral to pick up her award after
Christmas. Joanne later met and was photographed
with Queen Elizabeth II when the queen visited
Bloomsbury's headquarters.

⇃ WORLD PREMIERE ⇂

In spring 2001, as the Harry Potter books continued to
gain admirers worldwide, Warner Bros. started to ramp
up the hype for the first film. In June, the studio released
a full-length trailer. It opened with Hagrid asking Harry,
"You ever make anything happen? Anything you couldn't
explain?" It also included Harry's first flying lesson.

On November 4, 2001, a host of celebrities—including Cher, the Duchess of York, Sting, and Ben Stiller—joined Joanne Rowling and the actors in London for the world premiere of *Harry Potter and the Philosopher's Stone*. Fans loved it, but the reviews were not all favorable. Some critics felt that it stuck too closely to the book, so the plot did not work well as a movie. The film was a tremendous moneymaker for Warner Bros., however, and although it was very British in character, it had great appeal in the United States. Also, it catapulted all the books back to the top of the bestseller lists.

Comic Relief

In 2001, Joanne was invited to help Comic Relief, a popular charity that raises money through entertainment. On Red Nose Day, people buy and wear silly red noses, attend Comic Relief events, and watch comedy on TV, all to raise money to help vulnerable people. In March, Joanne published two 40-page books: *Quidditch Through the Ages* and *Fantastic Beasts and Where to Find Them*—both titles on the reading list for Hogwarts students. All the royalties went to Comic Relief, which received £6 million ($8.6 million) from sales of the books in that year alone. Joanne had achieved her own magical power: copies of any title she wrote flew out of the warehouses and off the bookshelves as fast as a disapparating wizard.

⋛ PRIVACY, PLEASE ⋛

Joanne was riding high on a wave of success, which meant endless media curiosity about her life. Once again, the newspapers intruded on her privacy. In early 2001, the press found out that she had a new boyfriend, a doctor named Neil Murray. Some people thought he looked like Harry Potter because he wore round glasses. In July, Neil joined Joanne and Jessica on vacation in Mauritius, an island in the Indian Ocean. Photographers followed them to secretly snap pictures with zoom lenses. The UK celebrity magazine *OK!* printed a photo including Jessica to accompany an article about the couple.

Joanne was furious. She went to the Press Complaints Commission (PCC) to complain about the magazine putting her daughter in the public eye. The PCC ruled in her favor, stating that the children of celebrity parents have a right to privacy.

⟩ A QUIET WEDDING ⟨

The romance was serious, and Joanne and Neil decided to marry. The couple knew they needed a secluded place to live, away from the constant gaze of the media. They found Killiechassie House, a beautiful country home in Scotland, and made plans for the wedding. To avoid prying eyes, the pair decided to get married at home. Joanne even went in disguise to buy her wedding dress, because she didn't want anyone to recognize her.

Joanne and Neil were married on December 26, 2001. For Joanne, it was a far happier event than her first wedding. The couple celebrated with a select group of fifteen guests, all close family and friends, including her father, Peter Rowling, and his second wife. Joanne had three bridesmaids—her sister, Di; Neil's sister Lorna; and Jessica. There was no chance for a honeymoon, though; Joanne had to push on with writing book five.

By now, Joanne was too well known in Edinburgh to be able to sit quietly in a café to work, so she wrote in an office at home. She and Neil settled down in Killiechassie and were mostly able to keep their lives private. In 2003, their son, David, was born, followed by a daughter, Mackenzie, in 2005.

HARRY POTTER AND THE ORDER OF THE PHOENIX

The fifth volume of Harry's story was offered to the world in June 2003. At 768 pages, it was the longest book many of its young readers had ever read. As the forces of Lord Voldemort grow stronger, Harry and his friends join the Order of the Phoenix, a secret group fighting the rise of dark wizardry.

Cartoon Jo

In 2003, Joanne had a cameo in an episode of the well-loved show *The Simpsons*. In the episode, set in England, the Simpsons family bumps into the author outside a bookstore. Lisa asks Joanne what happens at the end of the Harry Potter series. "He grows up and marries you," the author replies. "Is that what you want to hear?"

⋚ ACCUSED OF STEALING ⋚

At the start of the 2000s, Joanne faced a new challenge—this time, from another author. Nancy Stouffer claimed that Joanne stole the ideas from her books *The Legend of Rah and the Muggles* and *Larry Potter and His Best Friend Lilly*. The first has characters called Muggles—tiny people who look like babies—and the second features a hero, Larry Potter, who wears glasses and has a friend named Lilly. Harry Potter's mother is also named Lily. None of Stouffer's books include magic. Stouffer brought a plagiarism (copying) case against J. K. Rowling in 2002, which she lost. Joanne was relieved, but it had been a stressful experience.

Although she did not take her case to the courts, the science-fiction author Ursula Le Guin once mentioned that she thought Joanne should have acknowledged her 1968 novel *A Wizard of Earthsea* as an influence. The story is about a young magician called Ged; the wizard Ogion takes him away as a boy to study at a school of wizardry. Joanne maintains that, like every writer, she has absorbed ideas from others, but she has never deliberately copied anyone's work.

⋛ THE FINAL SHOWDOWN ⋛

Joanne continued writing the final long, complex, and increasingly dark titles in the series. In 2005, *Harry Potter and the Half-Blood Prince* came out, the story of how Hogwarts headmaster Dumbledore tries to prepare Harry to face Lord Voldemort.

The last book in the series was due for release in 2007. It would finish with the eagerly awaited dramatic showdown between Harry and his mortal enemy. By this time, excitement about how the story would end was so high that Joanne and Bloomsbury Publishing hatched a complicated plot to prevent the ending from being revealed before publication. Her editor,

Emma Matthewson, worked on a computer that was not connected to the internet, so hackers could not access her files. The first draft was given a code name, Edinburgh Potters, and only the small team reading the drafts knew about it.

Once the final draft was complete, it was vital to deliver it by hand in utmost secrecy. One evening, Joanne's agent, Christopher Little, invited Bloomsbury head Nigel Newton for a quiet drink. When he entered the bar, Nigel noticed that Christopher had a large superstore shopping bag by his feet—but neither of them mentioned that bag. The pair enjoyed a beer, and then Nigel walked out of the bar with the bag containing Joanne's final version of *Harry Potter and the Deathly Hallows.*

At home, Nigel quickly placed the first few pages of another manuscript on top so his wife wouldn't know what it was, and then stayed up all night to read it. The following morning, he drove it to Bloomsbury and handed it over safely to Emma Matthewson. Exhausted and relieved, Nigel's mission was over.

⋛ THE END OF HARRY POTTER? ⋛

As the Harry Potter phase of her life drew to a close, Joanne felt a mixture of emotions. She explained that finishing the series was "the most remarkable feeling I've ever had," and she felt both "euphoric and devastated"—very high and very low. Writing a chapter near the end brought her to tears. She had been planning the end of the story for so many years, and finally she was putting pen to paper. When she took out the carefully guarded final chapter and added it to the manuscript, ten years of work was over.

Of course, *Harry Potter and the Deathly Hallows* was immensely successful. With midnight book launches held worldwide, fifteen million copies were sold in the first twenty-four hours! It was the fastest-selling book ever. Yet Joanne vowed there would be no further Harry Potter titles.

CHAPTER 7

LIFE AFTER HARRY

As soon as she achieved major success and vast wealth, Joanne resolved to give generously to charities. Although she hated being in the public eye, she wanted to use her fame and fortune to help society. While she was still working on the Harry Potter series, she became involved in charitable work. She made her first significant donation of £500,000 ($760,000) in 2000 to the National Council for One Parent Families (later renamed Gingerbread). In September of that year, she became an ambassador for the charity, tasked with encouraging other people and organizations to donate money. Gingerbread campaigns on behalf of single-parent families and gives them practical support in day-to-day life.

⋝ FIGHTING TWICE AS HARD ⋜

Joanne knew firsthand how tough it could be as a single
mother, and she was determined to speak out about
her experiences. In an article for the popular British
newspaper *The Sun,* she explained how powerless she
had felt after the end of her first marriage. She was
already doing the job of two parents and desperately
wanted a paid position, too, to provide for her daughter.
But the cost of childcare made it impossible to go out
to work. It seemed to her that single moms "have to
fight twice as hard to get half as far" as mothers in two-
parent families.

Parents in Poverty

In the United States, 8 out of 10 single-parent families are headed by a woman. In 2018, about two-thirds of single mothers were working outside the home, according to the National Women's Law Center. Yet 40 percent of children with a working single mother were living in poverty. That's because childcare is so expensive that the mothers are usually forced to take low-paying jobs to fit around caring for their children.

In 2000, Joanne set up a charitable trust in her mother's maiden name, Volant, to support various causes working to reduce poverty in Scotland. Volant focuses on charities supporting women, children, and young people at risk—issues close to Joanne's heart.

Joanne wanted to help people with life-threatening conditions, too. For many people, being told by a doctor that they have cancer is one of their worst fears. Joanne became involved with Maggie's Centers after a friend was diagnosed with breast cancer. Maggie's Centers in Edinburgh offer counseling to

people with cancer and their families, talking to them as soon as they receive the diagnosis. The centers provide practical, emotional, and social support to people such as Isobel, who said, "The world hadn't changed, but cancer had totally changed who I was and I needed help to learn how to live again." To raise money for Maggie's Centers, Joanne gave book readings around Scotland and for several years was the charity's patron—a well-known person who supports the organization and lends their name to campaigns.

⋛ SUPPORTING PEOPLE WITH MS ⋚

Having witnessed her mother's multiple sclerosis, Joanne was intent on helping improve care for people with MS, which still has no cure. She started to work with the Multiple Sclerosis Society in Scotland, a country that has one of the highest rates of the disease. Joanne was its patron from 2000 to 2009 and lobbied the Scottish Parliament, trying to persuade politicians to give more support to people with MS.

In 2010, Joanne turned forty-five, the same age as her mother when she died. This prompted her to donate £10 million ($15.5 million) to the University of Edinburgh to found a charity to engage in MS research. The Anne Rowling Regenerative Neurology Clinic opened three years later. Princess Anne came to officially open the center. Alongside the princess, Joanne was given a tour, and they saw the excellent facilities for patients and their families. At the clinic, scientists conduct cutting-edge research into MS and similar diseases, support people who have received a diagnosis, and look for ways to repair damage to the body caused by MS.

Anne Rowling

⋛ LUMOS ⋜

Joanne also extended her charitable work abroad
by founding Lumos in 2005 to support the eight
million children living in orphanages around the world.
Eight out of every ten of those children have a living
parent, but their families are often so poor that they
cannot care for them. Joanne had of course written
extensively in the Harry Potter series about how it feels
to be a child with no place to call home. Lumos supports
families so they do not have to send their children to
institutions and helps young people in orphanages
return home. This support is provided by teachers,
social workers, and other caregivers.

⋝ BEEDLE THE BARD ⋜

Although Joanne was putting much of her energy
into charitable work, she continued writing, despite
her fear that none of her future work would ever be
as successful as the Harry Potter series. In 2007, she
wrote *The Tales of Beedle the Bard,* the book of fairy
tales that Hermione reads in *Harry Potter and the
Deathly Hallows,* searching for clues for how to defeat
Voldemort.

At first, Joanne hand-wrote only seven copies of the
book with her own illustrations and sent six of them
to people who had been especially helpful in creating
the Harry Potter books. The seventh copy was sold for
£1.95 million ($3.9 million) at an auction in London,
the highest price ever paid for a modern book. All the
money went to support Lumos.

After pressure from devoted fans to make *The
Tales of Beedle the Bard* available, it was printed and
published in 2008. Once more, Lumos benefited from
the profits, and the charity received £4.2 million
($7.9 million) from sales in the first week alone. It had
become remarkably easy for Joanne to raise money—
every title shepublished became a bestseller overnight.

THE WIZARDING WORLD

While Joanne was expanding her charitable work, Warner Bros. was seeking a way to extend the extraordinarily profitable world of Harry Potter once the final movie was released in 2011. In the United States, Universal Studios made an agreement with Warner Bros. to create a theme park.

The Wizarding World of Harry Potter opened in Orlando, Florida, in 2010. It re-creates the magical shops of Diagon Alley, offers underground journeys deep beneath Gringotts Bank, and takes visitors on roller-coaster rides into the Forbidden Forest to meet magical creatures.

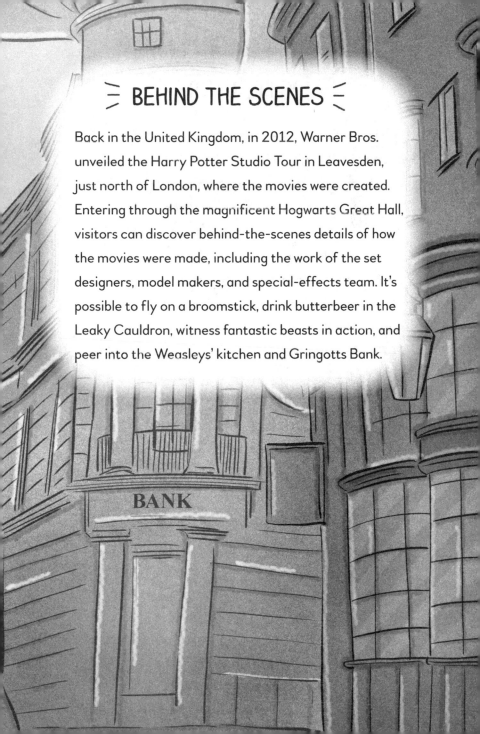

BEHIND THE SCENES

Back in the United Kingdom, in 2012, Warner Bros. unveiled the Harry Potter Studio Tour in Leavesden, just north of London, where the movies were created. Entering through the magnificent Hogwarts Great Hall, visitors can discover behind-the-scenes details of how the movies were made, including the work of the set designers, model makers, and special-effects team. It's possible to fly on a broomstick, drink butterbeer in the Leaky Cauldron, witness fantastic beasts in action, and peer into the Weasleys' kitchen and Gringotts Bank.

BANK

POTTERMORE

Few Harry Potter fans were able to travel to Orlando or London, though. Joanne realized that her followers were hungry for more information about Harry Potter from his creator, and she began work on a new secret project. In 2011, rumors abounded about what it would be. In June, Harry Potter fan sites began publishing coordinates to places on SecretStreetView.com. The site was owned by J. K. Rowling, and the places revealed hidden letters that spelled out the title: POTTERMORE. This was Joanne's own Harry Potter website.

Pottermore is now called Wizarding World. On it, Joanne writes articles related to Harry Potter's world: his family, the history of magic in North America, magical transport, the moving portraits, wizarding schools, and more. Fans can read news about J. K. Rowling, play games, and take quizzes. They can become virtual Hogwarts students, working through the books scene by scene and discovering new details about their favorite characters.

In 2019, the Wizarding World site released four ebooks. Based on Hogwarts lessons, they include:

→ A Journey Through Care of Magical Creatures

→ A Journey Through Charms and Defense Against the Dark Arts

→ A Journey Through Potions and Herbology

→ A Journey Through Divination and Astronomy

⋛ FANTASTIC BEASTS ⋚

The enthusiasm for Joanne's wizarding world was so
great that she decided to write more stories, even
though she had declared that Harry's adventures were
over. It was the loyalty of her fans and their passion for
all things Harry Potter that changed her mind.

Back in 2001, she had written *Fantastic Beasts and
Where to Find Them* for Comic Relief—a prequel to the
Harry Potter story (see page 109). In 2013, Warner
Bros. approached Joanne to ask if that book could be
turned into a movie. "I sat down to write some notes,
and [before I knew it], I'd written a story, and then that
story became a screenplay," she recalled. It was her
first movie script.

Joanne then set to work alongside the director,
David Yates. He found the story line very dark and
advised her to "lighten this up a little." They went
through many drafts until the story was ready for
filming. *Fantastic Beasts and Where to Find Them* was
released in 2016, and the second film, *Fantastic Beasts:
The Crimes of Grindelwald,* came out in 2018. They
starred British actor Eddie Redmayne as wizard Newt
Scamander. Three more films in the series are planned.

⋛ A NEW DIRECTION ⋚

Back in her twenties, Joanne had worked on two adult novels that never became published books. Now she could write whatever she wanted, and people would rush to read it.

Her first adult title was *The Casual Vacancy* (2012). The idea came to her while she was on a plane in the United States on a book tour to promote *Harry Potter and the Deathly Hallows*. Joanne realized there is something about traveling that seems to fire her imagination. As with Harry Potter, it was a story she felt she just had to write.

The story focuses on the "pretty little town of Pagford," a made-up town in the West of England. Under the surface of this seemingly happy world lurk deep problems involving differences of class and race, alongside poverty and hidden abuse. Joanne had not forgotten her experience of poverty and hoped to show how being treated badly because of a low income or family situation could have terrible effects on a person's life.

Reviews were mixed, but Joanne did not mind—she had written the book she wanted to write. The book reached number one on the Amazon book chart within hours of its release. In 2015, it was adapted into a three-part miniseries on the US TV network HBO and on the BBC in the United Kingdom.

In 2013, Joanne devised an experiment. She published a detective novel, *The Cuckoo's Calling*, under the pseudonym Robert Galbraith to hide her identity. Joanne was curious to see how the book would be judged as if written by an unknown author.

The novel follows the fortunes of Cormoran Strike, a former soldier running a private-detective firm. As usual, Joanne's characters are interesting and unusual. Strike is tough but damaged, both physically and mentally, by his wartime experiences. His bold assistant, Robin, is new to detective work, yet dedicated and willing to take risks.

The Cuckoo's Calling had sold just 1,500 copies when someone at Joanne's lawyers' company leaked the author's true identity to a friend, who informed the British *Sunday Times*. Within hours, the title raced to the top of Amazon's sales list.

Joanne was angry, explaining that she was "yearning to . . . work without hype or expectation and to receive totally unvarnished feedback." With everyone knowing the real author, "Mr. Galbraith" had published four Cormoran Strike books by 2018, with more planned.

⇒ HARRY POTTER ONSTAGE ⇐

Joanne had not forgotten Harry Potter, though. In 2015, she wrote a brand-new story for the theater, set nineteen years after the final book. Playwright Jack Thorne adapted her tale into a play: *Harry Potter and the Cursed Child*. In it, Harry is married with three children and a hectic job at the Ministry of Magic. You might think that all his troubles are in the past, but history still weighs heavily on him, and it affects his youngest son, Albus.

The plot was shrouded in secrecy, and the organizers promoted a #KeepTheSecrets slogan to encourage the audience to keep the plot twists to themselves. In contrast to the critics' mixed response to the movies, by 2019, the play had won more prizes than any other in the history of the Olivier Awards.

For the London production of *Harry Potter and the Cursed Child,* Noma Dumeweni, a black actress, was cast as Hermione. Joanne was pleased, saying that she had never spelled out Hermione's race. However, the casting raised the issue of diversity in the series once again. Joanne has responded to critics by explaining that there are minority ethnic and LGBTQ+ characters throughout. In 2007, for example, she announced that Albus Dumbledore was gay and as a young man had a loving relationship with Gellert Grindelwald. When asked if any Jewish students attended Hogwarts, she pointed to Anthony Goldstein, a Ravenclaw wizard who joined Dumbledore's Army. But these examples are not clear in the books. As the original ideas spin off in new directions, Joanne and the creative teams are making adjustments to ensure that the characters more closely reflect our diverse society.

⋛ PRIVATE AND PUBLIC ⋚

J. K. Rowling is the highest-earning author in the world. With all her income from the books, films, plays, and spinoffs, she makes about £6 million ($7.5 million) per day. Naturally, she now lives an extremely comfortable life. As well as her country mansion, Killiechassie House, she owns a townhouse in fashionable Kensington, London. But Joanne continues to donate much of her wealth to charitable causes. She could easily be on the list of the world's billionaires, but she dropped off the list in 2018, owing to her generous donations to charity.

In 2020, Joanne released a serialized fairy tale called "The Ickabog" for free online, as a way to help children get through difficult times during the COVID-19 pandemic.

Since 2014, Joanne has been based in Scotland and maintains her privacy to protect her husband and three children. But she is a public figure, engaging with her fans via the Wizarding World website, and she is active on Twitter, discussing Harry Potter characters and the social issues that are close to her heart. J. K. Rowling might have thought that the Harry Potter stage of her life was almost over as she unlocked the safe containing the final chapter of *Deathly Hallows*. Yet it seems Harry Potter will remain a central part of her world for the rest of her life.

CONCLUSION

INSPIRING READERS AND WRITERS

J. K. Rowling's work has had a unique effect on many aspects of culture and business. But perhaps it has had the greatest effect on children's reading and love of literature.

Bloomsbury's deal with Joanne transformed it from a small company into one of the most successful children's publishers. The film series was remarkably profitable for Warner Bros. All eight movies became top-grossing films at the box office, making a massive £1.9 billion ($2.4 billion).

Other companies have become wealthy through the Harry Potter franchises, too. A franchise means a company has permission to use a business's trade name. Several stores have brought out Harry Potter clothing lines, and the franchise has also been a winner for toy companies such as Mattel and Hasbro, making soft toys, action figures, and board games. If dedicated fans can save up $400, they can even buy a 6,000-piece LEGO set to build their own Hogwarts Castle.

⟩ GREAT FOR GAMERS ⟨

With dramatic scenes and action involving magic,
monsters, and flying, the Harry Potter stories inspired
an array of computer games. In 2019, the company
behind Pokémon Go released the Wizards Unite
augmented-reality game for phones and tablets.
Players are challenged to hunt for "foundables"—
objects, creatures, and memories from the Harry
Potter and Fantastic Beasts titles. They then cast spells
and return the foundables to the wizarding world, where
they belong.

MUGGLE TOURISM

In Britain, the tourist industry makes the most of its English-born wizard to promote trips to the United Kingdom. The Warner Bros. Studio Tour is a popular attraction. Fans from across the globe who grew up relishing every Harry Potter book travel to London to wander around the movie sets and remember their favorite scenes. The tour is even offered in Mandarin for Chinese visitors.

Tourists also like to visit other places associated with J. K. Rowling, including Edinburgh, where she completed the first few books, and the Wye Valley. Guides lead fans on walks around the Wye region to visit Tutshill and enjoy the beautiful landscape of Joanne's childhood.

The movie locations attract sightseers, too. The VisitEngland tourist website has a "Muggle's guide to Harry Potter filming locations," which includes the magnificent Christ Church College, Oxford. In the films, Harry, Ron, and Hermione walk up the impressive stairway when they first arrive at Hogwarts, in awe of their new surroundings, and the college's Great Hall inspired the Hogwarts dining hall.

QUIDDITCH: FROM FANTASY TO REALITY

Muggle Quidditch has become a real sport, too! The goalposts are often Hula-Hoops on posts, anchored firmly to the ground. The Quaffle is frequently a slightly deflated volleyball, while Bludgers are dodgeballs. Without magical wings, the Golden Snitch is a simple tennis ball in a sock, tucked into the shorts of a Muggle. The Seeker snatches the sock to finish the game.

⋜ A LITERARY LEGEND ⋜

Movies, games, and attractions aside, for Harry Potter followers worldwide, the stories themselves remain the focus. Fans endlessly discuss the characters, plots, and theories about the wizarding world on multiple websites, while news about Harry Potter–related events, movies, and merchandise appears on sites such as Mugglenet.com. The Harry Potter YouTube channel contains the biggest collection of licensed movie clips and has over 72 million Facebook fans.

Joanne's followers care deeply about the characters in the stories. Every year on May 2, the anniversary of the Battle of Hogwarts in the final book, Joanne apologizes for the death of one of the characters that upset her fans. They are willing to forgive her, though; they adore her so much that they call her "the queen."

Despite her wealth and fame, Joanne still interacts regularly with her fans. Young people who are depressed or being bullied reach out to her on Twitter, and she offers support. One follower got in touch because that person had lost all hope in the world, and Joanne responded with beautiful photos from nature, saying, "The world is full of wonderful things you

haven't seen yet. Don't ever give up on the chance of seeing them."

As Joanne shares her birthday with Harry, bakers around the world make cakes to celebrate her special day, featuring scenes from the stories.

⋛ A LOVE OF LITERATURE ⋜

J. K. Rowling's main impact has been on reading. Sales of Harry Potter books continue to grow, the stories inspiring millions of children to read. The tales help many young readers cope with their challenges, fears, and even the concept of death. They have encouraged adults to read children's books, too, bringing wider attention to children's literature.

Although the main character is a boy, the Harry Potter stories have positive messages for girl readers through strong, independent female characters—

not only Hermione. Luna shows heroic courage and calmness, even when trapped in a cellar by the ruthless Malfoys, while Professor McGonagall risks her life to stand up to the bloodthirsty Death Eaters. Ginny develops from a shy, quiet child to become rebellious and fearless, a key member of the group fighting Voldemort. These characters are inspiring role models.

"Anyone who can persuade children to read should be treasured."
—Charlie Griffiths, director of the UK National Literacy Association

How Many Books?

→ About 500 million copies of Harry Potter titles have been printed worldwide. On average, 1 in every 15 people in the world owns a Harry Potter book.

→ The books have been published in 80 languages.

→ By 2018, about 120 million copies of *Harry Potter and the Philosopher's Stone* had been sold worldwide.

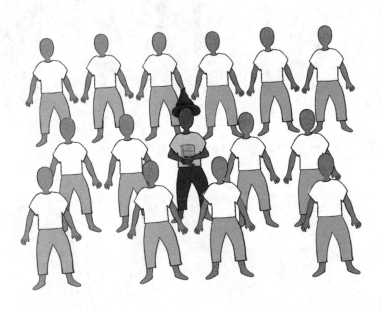

Joanne says that her personal favorites out of all the books she has written are *Harry Potter and the Sorcerer's Stone*, *Harry Potter and the Deathly Hallows*, and *The Casual Vacancy*.

⹀ BUDDING WRITERS ⹀

J. K. Rowling has greatly motivated others to write. Many authors developed their love of reading when they became drawn into Harry Potter's world. While they were hooked on the books, they were absorbing lessons about writing—developing their imaginations and learning how to bring in humor and how to draw characters together to unite against common enemies.

"Before I ever thought of becoming a writer, J. K. Rowling made me a reader." —V. E. Schwab, *A Conjuring of Light*

"She gave [me] permission to be funny even when things got dark." —Adrienne Kress, *The Explorers: The Door in the Alley*

IMAGINATION AND DETERMINATION

What can we learn from Joanne even if we are
not writers? When she made a speech at Harvard
University in 2008, she talked about the importance of
imagination, "the power that enables us to empathize
with humans whose experiences we have never shared."
Imagination allows us to think about others and do
good in the world.

Joanne has a message of determination as well. She
remembers that her life was in pieces seven years after
she finished university. Yet, she also remembers this:

<u>Timeline</u>

July 31
Joanne Rowling is born in Yate, near Bristol, in England.

June 28
Joanne's sister, Dianne Rowling, is born.

The Rowling family moves to Tutshill in the Forest of Dean.

1965   1967   1974

Joanne's family moves to Winterbourne, near Bristol.

Joanne's grandmother Kathleen dies.

Joanne thinks up the Harry Potter story on a train journey.

December 30
Joanne's mother dies.

October 16
Joanne marries Jorge Arantes.

1990   1991 1992

Joanne moves to Manchester.

Joanne goes to Portugal to teach English.

Joanne starts secondary school at Wyedean Comprehensive.

Joanne spends a year in Paris as part of her schooling.

1976 1983 1985 1987

Joanne goes to the University of Exeter.

Joanne graduates from Exeter. She takes a secretarial course and moves to London to work as a secretary.

July 27
Joanne and Jorge's daughter, Jessica, is born.

August
Bloomsbury agrees to publish the first Harry Potter book.

June 26
Harry Potter and the Philosopher's Stone is published in the United Kingdom.

1993 1995 1996 1997

November
Joanne and Jorge split up, and Joanne and Jessica later move to Scotland.

August
Joanne starts a teacher-training course.

Joanne wins her first book prize, the Nestlé Smarties Book Prize Gold Medal.

September
Harry Potter and the Sorcerer's Stone is published in the US.

Joanne sets up Volant, a charitable trust to help causes working to reduce poverty.

1998   1999   2000

Joanne and Jessica move to Hazelbank Terrace, Edinburgh.

Joanne goes on a book tour of the US.

The Warner Bros. Studio Tour in Leavesden is opened to the public.

2010   2012

Joanne donates money to found a charity to research multiple sclerosis. The Wizarding World of Harry Potter opens in Orlando, Florida.

Joanne's first book written for adults, *The Casual Vacancy,* is published.

November 4
The film *Harry Potter and the Philosopher's Stone* premieres.

March 24
Joanne and Neil's son, David, is born.

2001   2003   2005

December 26
Joanne marries Neil Murray at home at Killiechassie House.

January 23
Joanne and Neil's daughter, Mackenzie, is born. Joanne founds Lumos, a charity to support children living in orphanages worldwide.

Joanne publishes her first Cormoran Strike novel under the name Robert Galbraith.

The first film in the Fantastic Beasts series is released.

2013 2015 2016 2019

The stage play *Harry Potter and the Cursed Child* opens.

Wizarding World publishes four ebooks based on Hogwarts lessons.

Further Reading

→ *J. K. Rowling: Author of the Harry Potter Series* by Jennifer Hunsicker (Capstone, 2017)

→ *Who Is J. K. Rowling?* by Pam Pollack and Meg Belviso (Grosset & Dunlap, 2012)

→ *Work It, Girl: Boss the Bestseller List Like J. K. Rowling* by Caroline Moss (Frances Lincoln Children's Books, 2019)

Websites

→ jkrowling.com
The official website of author J. K. Rowling, with news and updates.

→ wizardingworld.com
Information, games, and activities about Harry Potter and the wizarding world.

<u>Glossary</u>

advance: In publishing, a sum of money an author receives before their book is published.

agent: A person whose job is to find a company that will publish a writer's work.

ban: To forbid or prohibit something, such as the sale of a book.

boarding school: A school where children can live during the school year.

classic (book): Accepted as one of the best or most important of its kind.

contract: A written agreement.

counseling: Advice from an expert about a problem.

Glossary

depression: A mood disorder. People with depression may feel sad and hopeless all the time and find it hard to carry out day-to-day activities.

diagnose: To identify an illness or condition from its signs and symptoms.

diversity: A variety of people who are different from one another (such as people of different races or cultures).

fantasy: A story with magic and adventure, especially in a setting that is not the real world.

feminist: A person who believes that women should have the same rights and opportunities that men have.

graduate: To get an academic degree from a university or other school.

Glossary

human rights abuses: Violations of the basic rights of people by treating them unfairly or cruelly.

immune system: The system in the body that fights infection and disease.

launch (book): An event to celebrate the publication of a new book.

manuscript: A book written by an author, before it is edited and printed.

merchandise: Items for sale, such as T-shirts, posters, and toys, that are linked to a particular book, movie, TV show, video game, or the like.

national service: The system in some countries in which people between certain ages must do military training or service for a specified period.

Glossary

royalty: A sum of money that an author earns when their books are sold.

typewriter: A machine that prints text, in use before computers. It has keys that are pressed to make metal letters strike a piece of paper through a strip of inked cloth.

welfare benefits: Money or other help, such as housing, given by the government to people who need it.

Index

Index

Index

Index

Index

FOLLOW THE TRAIL!

TURN THE PAGE FOR A SNEAK PEEK AT THESE TRAILBLAZERS BIOGRAPHIES!

TRAIL BLAZERS
MARTIN LUTHER KING JR.
FIGHTING FOR CIVIL RIGHTS
I have a dream...
CHRISTINE PLATT

Early in the civil rights movement, black people made up the majority of Martin's supporters, but by the 1960s, Martin had won over the hearts and minds of many white people as well. Although this was a great success for the movement, those who were against equal rights for black people saw this as problematic. It was not uncommon for Martin to receive hate letters in the mail or threatening phone calls in which people vowed to kill him and his family. Sometimes Martin was even harassed by the police in a city he was visiting.

Police Brutality

For several decades following the abolition of slavery, only white men were allowed to serve on the police force. Many police officers were former Confederate soldiers and members of hate groups that discriminated against black people. They often abused their power by threatening, intimidating, and even killing black people. This violence continued throughout the civil rights movement even in the midst of peaceful protests. In modern America, there continue to be reasons for black communities to distrust some police officers, and organizations such as Black Lives Matter have formed to seek justice.

On October 19, 1960, Martin was among over fifty protesters taking part in a department store sit-in. Located in Atlanta, Rich's department store had a special room called the Magnolia Room. Even though black people could purchase items from Rich's, only white people could sit in the Magnolia Room and try on the clothes in there. When Martin and the other protesters entered the Magnolia Room and refused to leave, the police arrested them. Eventually everyone was released—except Martin.

Martin was the last leader to speak, and his speech would resonate with listeners all over the globe. It remains one of the most quoted speeches of all time.

After Martin's speech, A. Philip Randolph asked the crowd to take a pledge to commit to the struggle and support the fight against segregation and racism.

I pledge my heart and my mind and my body unequivocally and without regard to personal sacrifice, to the achievement of social peace through social justice.

The crowd responded with a resounding, "I do pledge!" The March on Washington concluded with one of Martin's first mentors, Morehouse College President Dr. Benjamin E. Mays, giving a blessing. Then, in a beautiful moment of solidarity, the crowd joined together to sing the anthem of the civil rights movement, "We Shall Overcome."

Following the success of the march, President Kennedy scheduled a meeting with the Big Ten and other march leaders immediately afterward. The group met him at the White House, and he congratulated them on the peaceful demonstration. As the march had been so well attended and successful, President Kennedy hoped it would improve the chances that Congress would support his civil rights act.

TRAILBLAZERS
SIMONE BILES
GOLDEN GIRL OF GYMNASTICS
We can push ourselves further!
SALLY J. MORGAN

It's a moment I'll feel forever.... I'm excited about the whole team being together to start training.

There was a tradition for the women's artistic gymnastics team to give themselves a name. The 2012 Olympic team had called themselves the Fierce Five. Simone and the other girls agreed on the Final Five, both in honor of the fact that they would be the last team coached by Márta Károlyi, who had announced that she would retire after the games, and because they would be the last team of five to compete. The plan was that for the 2020 Olympic Games onward, teams for women's gymnastics would shrink to four, but starting in 2024, teams will have five gymnasts again.

The Final Five

Along with Simone Biles, these gymnasts made up the Final Five:

GABBY DOUGLAS (See page 72)

LAURIE HERNANDEZ
Born: June 9, 2000
At 16 years old, Laurie was the youngest member of the Final Five. The 2016 Olympics was her first major international competition.
Star events: balance beam and an expressive floor routine

MADISON KOCIAN

Born: June 15, 1997

Madison won gold at the 2015 national championships on uneven bars and tied for first at the world championships in the same event. Madison was specially selected for the Olympics to give the team the best chance at achieving a medal in this event.

Star event: uneven bars

ALY RAISMAN (See page 73)

Simone had qualified for the team in first place, but a stumble on beam showed she still had work to do if she wanted to be sure of gold. She would have to improve quickly—they were due to fly to Rio in just sixteen days.

TRAIL BLAZERS
JANE GOODALL
A LIFE WITH CHIMPS
Every individual matters.
ANITA GANERI

Primate, Monkey, or Ape?

There are more than three hundred species of primates. They all share many features, including large brains compared to the size of their bodies, forward-facing eyes, and flexible limbs and hands for grasping. But, while monkeys and apes (chimps, bonobos, gorillas, orangutans, and gibbons) are both primates, monkeys are not the same as apes. Here's how to tell them apart:

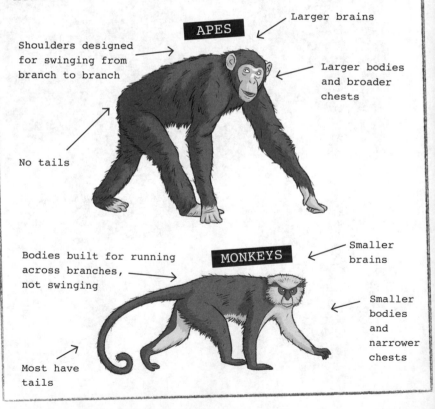

APES

Larger brains

Shoulders designed for swinging from branch to branch

Larger bodies and broader chests

No tails

MONKEYS

Smaller brains

Bodies built for running across branches, not swinging

Smaller bodies and narrower chests

Most have tails

Over the next few months, Jane's frustration grew. Sometimes, she didn't see any chimps for days, and when she did, she couldn't get close enough to observe them properly. So as not to startle the chimps, Jane wore clothes that blended in with the forest, and sat patiently for hours. The minute she tried to move nearer, the chimps scampered off. She was getting worried that if she didn't get results soon, Louis would have to cancel the project, and she would have to leave Gombe.

Sweater

Food and drink

BEANS

BEANS

Notebook and pens

Binoculars

Sleeping bag

Bagged lunch

COMING SOON . . .

Amelia Earhart

Lin-Manuel Miranda

"This is one of the finest practical guides for planning a good death that I have ever seen. Meyers is direct and his analyses, forged during twenty-years of pastoral practice in the clinical setting, are balanced and realistic. *A Good Death* could profit everyone, from doctors and nurses to families and students. It is superb."

Richard A. McCormick, S.J.
University of Notre Dame

"*A Good Death* is compassionately written, based on the author's knowledge and pastoral experiences. We are made aware of the ethical controversies that surround end-of-life care and the decisions we are free to make, as well as the dilemmas we face in this age of technology. I found the chapter on 'How to Get a Good Death' most interesting."

Julia A. Quinlan
Co-Founder, "Karen Ann Quinlan Hospice"

"The style of *A Good Death* is clear and persuasive; the tone is compassionate. The length is short: an obvious blessing. Charles Meyer explains how death occurs and argues that the quality of death depends on informed choice. His chapter on the role of spirituality should be required reading before visiting the dying. His use of humor reminds us that, while death is serious, it need not be grim."

Denise Lardner Carmody
Santa Clara University

"This is one of the finest books on death and dying that I have read. In it, Charles Meyer provides a treasure trove of information and practical guidelines to help us 'do' death well, or at least better. In a clear, succinct, very readable style, he addresses such topics as health care changes, treatment options, legal and ethical issues, and the role of spirituality in the dying process."

Sandra DeGidio, OSM, Author
Praying With the Sick

"Charles Meyer has graced us with a gentle but powerful little book marked by practical wisdom, care, and sensitivity. I found reading *A Good Death* not only extremely informative but calming and a 'healing' experience. Meyer shows us the importance of comfort and healing once we are beyond cure. Another marvelous book from Twenty-Third."

Dick Westley, Author
When It's Right to Die, Redemptive Intimacy

"Meyer combines his brilliance as an author with his awareness and presence as chaplain and priest to speak forthrightly and lovingly about not only the possibility of 'a good death' but pathways to realize it in our own lives and in the lives of those we love. "

Rev. Richard B. Gilbert
Executive Director, The World Pastoral Care Center

"It is unusual to find a delightfully written and not-at-all morbid discussion of dealing with one's impending death or the death of a loved one. As I tell my medical and law students, people did manage to die before lawyers were invented, and Charles Meyer's book will go a long way toward restoring balance to the process."

Angela R. Holder, LL.M.
Clinical Professor of Pediatrics, Yale University

"Meyer's discussion of the difference between 'healing' and 'curing' and the possibilities for healing in the dying process is extremely well done. This is a concept that both professionals and the public need help in understanding."

Mary L. Meyer
Director, Program Department, Choice in Dying

"This book simplifies the bewildering and overwhelming maze that patients and families often face at the end of life. It challenges readers to broach end-of-life issues with loved ones and equips them to make informed decisions about what a good death means."

Marjorie Mulanax
Executive Director, Hospice Austin

"Chaplain Meyer has written a resource that should prove very helpful to people who are wrestling with end-of-life issues (or should be) and who desire a clear, concise exposition of the major issues involved.

"A strength of this book is the chapter on the role of spirituality, an excellent treatment of a very complex topic, written in a succinct and readable manner. Although not theologically profound, his exposition of the issues involved and his patient-centered approach to dealing with this often touchy subject represent a genuine contribution."

Stephen Sapp, Ph.D.
Editor, *Journal of Religious Gerontology*
University of Miami

A
GOOD
DEATH

Challenges
Choices
and
Care Options

CHARLES MEYER

TWENTY-THIRD PUBLICATIONS
Mystic, CT 06355

Dedication

With thanks to the patients, families,
nurses, and physicians
who have taught me the meaning of a good death.

Twenty-Third Publications
185 Willow Street
P.O. Box 180
Mystic, CT 06355
(860) 536-2611
800-321-0411

ISBN 0-89622-923-8
Library of Congress Catalog Card Number 98-60132
Printed in the U.S.A.

CONTENTS

95788

INTRODUCTION

What two things would provide a good death for you?

In presentations around the country I've asked this question of thousands of people, and regardless of the age group, I consistently get the same answers. The Big Four responses are: 1) quick, 2) painless, 3) at home, and 4) surrounded by family. Others have added: not scared, remembered, guilt free, spiritually aligned with God, and before my children. A little further afield are: not on the day I win the lottery, pleasantly confused, cheap, and after sex and chocolate (not necessarily in that order). Organ bank workers responded: with all my parts so I can donate them. A convention of funeral directors wanted to die prepared. Office nurses said: by appointment only.

The Big Four, as well as all these others, indicate that people want to die with a large degree of comfort and control. So it's interesting to contrast our definition of a good death with the reality of where it actually occurs. Although we repeatedly assert that we want our death to be quick, painless, at home, and with family around, *eighty-five percent* of deaths in this country occur in medical settings (hospitals, nursing homes, skilled facilities); *fifteen percent* of that eighty-five die in intensive care units. Hospital deaths are seldom quick or painless; families are kept at bay by unreasonable visiting restrictions, patients are obviously not at home surrounded by familiar belongings or their favorite pet nuzzling their neck.

How do we explain this incredible disparity between what

we say we want and what we actually get? Though there are many parts to this issue, the major one is that most of us are unfamiliar with *how we die*. Our elders (people in their eighties or nineties) are the last repository of information about how people used to die. In 1950, over fifty percent of deaths occurred at home. Intensive Care Units hadn't been invented yet; neither had ventilators, balloon pumps for cardiac bypass, TPN to dissolve clots, CT scanners, Magnetic Resonance Imaging machines (MRI), or stereotactic mammography. So our elders kept people at home, made them as comfortable as possible, often with a house call from their physician for morphine, and provided family care until the loved one died. Children were taught by experience and example how people died and what was to be done as death approached.

Over the last fifty years, incredible advances in technology, pharmacology, and surgery have convinced us that the only place permissible to die is in a hospital. We have moved from Marcus Welby to Chicago Hope and E.R. Have you ever noticed that neither of the latter shows has either a chaplain or a cashier? Both shows (and others like them) educate millions of Americans about what to expect from their healthcare system: free, maximum treatment from which the majority of people recover. Furthermore, the one thing that is never shown on these programs is the one thing about which Americans most need to be educated. They never show *how we die*. And they never portray home deaths.

The intent of this book is to do both; it clearly describes how we are supposed to die, and it compares home death with hospital death in order to offer choices for the patient and family. It is neither a defense of dying at home nor a critique of hospitals and doctors. It is an examination of how we *do* death with guidelines for how to get the kind of good death we say we want, whether at home or in a clinical setting. It briefly looks at changes in healthcare, explores exactly how we die and the value of medical interventions, discusses alternatives to current requirements for high-tech death, evaluates euthanasia and assisted suicide, questions traditional spiritual approaches to death, and offers specific suggestions for a good death and how to get one.

I've been a hospital chaplain and administrator for twenty years. In that time I've seen the changes in the way we do death. Today, patients are better informed. Middle-aged Baby Boomers are being confronted with death/dying issues. Ethics committees are assisting more with policies, and physicians themselves are aging. These facts should, in fact, move us in the direction of a good death or at least a better one. But those are generic statistical deaths, not yours and mine. The only way you and I will get the kind of death we want for ourselves and our loved ones is to determine exactly what it is and put things in place to assure that our wishes will be honored.

I hope this book will help do that.

Charles Meyer
Austin, Texas

1

CHANGES IN HEALTHCARE

"Just as the Holy Roman Empire was neither Holy, Roman, nor an Empire, the American Healthcare System is neither healthy, caring, nor a system." So said Walter Cronkite. But the good news is that we are beginning to see evidence of change in at least four areas involving healthcare.

1. From Optional to Obligatory

Healthcare (and deathcare) used to be viewed as the privilege available only to those who could afford it. Hospitals and wards were in fact invented to serve the indigent or needy who could not pay for a private physician to attend them in their homes. Labor unions fought for and won healthcare packages at the same time as the rest of the civilized world was instituting national systems of healthcare to cover all their citizens.

Today many people believe tying healthcare to employment is an anachronism. We are beginning to see healthcare as the obligation of a caring society. How we will provide it is not yet clear. Proposals range from government sponsored national healthcare to a single-payer system where healthcare corporations compete for the government dollar in the areas of treatment outcomes, customer satisfaction, and cost.

As this change occurs, there will be a much broader provision of care for hospice services both at home and in facilities specifically designed for comfort care. There will also be increased restrictions on treatment that is considered futile.

2. From "Imperative" to "Necessary"

We used to practice medicine and deliver healthcare under what was called the technological imperative. We believed that if we had the technology, we were required to use it. If you came into the ER and needed a ventilator, we put you on it. If you needed dialysis and we had the machine, we hooked you up to it. If you needed cardiopulmonary resuscitation (CPR), or artificial nutrition and hydration (AN/H), or antibiotics, or ICU admission, and we had the technology, we thought we were ethically required to provide it to you.

But now we are facing huge demographic changes that are making us examine the ethical allocation of these resources. For example: there are more people over age 65 in the U.S. than there are under age 20; the fastest growing age group is 85 and over; there are over 60,000 Americans 100 years old or older.

With the aging of America and the Baby Boomers coming into the system in huge numbers, we are now starting to ask when it is appropriate to offer a ventilator to someone, when it is ethically required not to do CPR or give antibiotics, when Intensive Care is excessive care.

The problem is that we have not yet learned that we don't have to do "everything possible" for persons who are in a terminal condition. We are required to do what is technically necessary to maintain the quality of life acceptable to the patient. It is because we are in this learning curve that many conflicts around end-of-life treatment arise between families and physicians. As we move away from physicians trained under the technological imperative and families who have grown up expecting it, our deathcare will become more humane and reasonable.

3. From Costly to Cost-Effective

With healthcare costs increasing annually at double the rate of inflation, the government tried a few years ago to offer reform—but was soundly defeated. The American public did not trust the President or the Congress to manage healthcare, and, as a result, we are seeing far more radical and deeper change than either the Republicans or Democrats could have imagined.

We are seeing the "corporatization" of healthcare; large healthcare corporations are purchasing or managing smaller systems. In the coming few years, there will be about five or six such conglomerates managing every healthcare bed in the country, including nursing homes, skilled nursing, and home healthcare. They may even run their own medical schools.

The upside of this is that competition should lead the system to be, for the very first time ever in history, cost effective. (In the eighties we didn't watch cost; we raised prices.) Now nationwide systems like Columbia/HCA, Tenet, and others are involved in measuring outcomes: patient, physician, and employee satisfaction with services, patient outcomes, speed of service delivery, use of supplies and relationship of salaries, wages, and benefits to patient days. The downside is that until the cost and employee ratio targets are balanced with quality measures, there will be a tendency to be too lean and service may suffer.

But for those of us involved in deathcare, the emphasis on futility or benefit of treatment will be a vast improvement that will lead to better comfort care that is both appropriate for the patient and cost effective for the system. Large systems will then make these the best practice standard for their entire system, enhancing terminal care across the country and rewarding innovative deathcare programs.

4. From Paternalism to Collaboration

Gone are the days when you gave your soul to Jesus and your body to your doctor. First of all the Boomers are entering the system, so the same people that took over the Dean's office in 1968 are going to take over the doctor's office, only it's a lot worse now. In the sixties the Boomers just *thought* they knew everything; now they *know* they know everything.

They've clicked their mouse and downloaded volumes of information about their disease and are coming into the system wondering why the doctors and hospitals don't know what they know about what works and what doesn't, including so-called "alternative" medicines and treatments. But increasing numbers of elders are also clicking mouses and are experiencing the currently required high-tech deaths of their friends. They are joining forces with their Boomer kids in saying "Hell NO, We Won't GO!" Not by high-tech, anyway.

As paternalism changes to collaboration we can expect more involvement of patients/families in end-of-life treatment, more demands and negotiation regarding code status, and much more dialogue about outcomes of what many regard as futile treatment.

Most of us grew up under a system of optional healthcare, practiced under the assumption of the technological imperative, dispensed in independent community hospitals by paternalistic practitioners. We are moving to a system where some level of healthcare is a societal obligation, providing what is technically necessary to sustain a high quality (not quantity) life, dispensed by cost-effective corporations to patients and families in collaboration with their physicians.

We are in the midst of the transition dealing with physicians, families, patients, and institutions who have one foot in each place, trying to figure out the right thing to do. As we move from the old to the new and advance up the learning curve, it is extremely important to understand the basic facts about how we die.

2

HOW WE DIE

Before 1950, over fifty percent of deaths occurred at home. Since then, technology, medicines, and treatment techniques have increased in number geometrically as their effectiveness has improved exponentially. We invented machines to supplant the function of organs and organ systems, developed intensive care units and special labs in which to use and support them, and discovered ways to merge computer technology with optics and lasers. All of these things were initially developed to be used with sick people who would eventually get better and no longer need them.

Ventilators would breathe for persons having had lung surgery or for premature infants whose lungs were not quite fully developed, but eventually both would regain lung function and not need the machine. Artificial hydration and nutrition tubes were to be used in post-surgical patients who could not swallow, but who would regain that ability and have the tubes removed. The balloon pump necessary for cardiac bypass surgery was to be a temporary method of keeping blood circulating while the heart was stopped, but would be turned off when the normal heart function returned.

But as our love affair with technology deepened we began to believe we were required to use it in *every* circumstance. If we could stave off death temporarily while the body was recovering from disease or surgery, maybe we could do it permanently. We then crossed the line from employing technology as a *temporary crutch* (to temporarily support the life of the patient, allowing the body to regain its natural functions), and increasingly began to use it to prolong bodily functions as long as possible, regardless of the organ systems collapsing around the one that was now taken over by a machine.

Prolonging the Process

We began to use the newly developed machinery and seemingly miraculous medicines not just to sustain life but to prolong dying. Instead of seeing death as the natural, normal, expected outcome of overwhelming disease or accident (or simply old age) as our grandparents did, we medicalized death and began treating it as one more illness to be conquered by overwhelming it with vast amounts of medicine, time, and technology in an acute care institution or intensive care unit.

This chapter will attempt to de-medicalize death, explain how we die, and offer options for a good death, or at least a better one than the current high-tech standard.

Is death terminal? Of course it is, but being terminal doesn't always mean you're dying. This is an important distinction. The question to ask regarding treatment decisions is, "Is the patient in a terminal condition?" Now we've all heard the fatuous comment that "life is a terminal condition" and that is true. With the possible exception of Elvis, the death rate on this planet is 100%. One out of one dies. Life is a sexually transmitted disease that is fatal. But families will often use this notion as an excuse to prolong useless treatments.

Doctor: "Your father is dying."
Family member (usually from out of town): "We're *all* dying. Keep the ventilator going."
Doctor: "But it's not benefiting him in any way."
Family member: "I'm a lawyer." *Doctor:* "Right."

Fortunately, many states now have a legal description of a "terminal condition" as a part of their Natural Death Act, or Death with Dignity laws. With variations it is something like this: A "terminal condition" is an incurable or irreversible condition caused by accident, injury, or disease, certified by two physicians, in which the provision of treatment would only artificially prolong the moment of death, and with which the patient would die in a short time without the continuation of life-sustaining treatment.

You will note that this does not mean you have one foot over the grave and the other on a banana peel. It does not mean you are *actively dying*. It means that your condition is *incurable* or *irreversible*, that regardless of what we do, we cannot cure the condition or reverse its trajectory toward death. The "short time" requirement is usually considered to be six months to a year. This definition covers not only people in hospitals or nursing homes on ventilators, dialysis, nutrition/hydration tubes, and various medications, it also covers persons with debilitating strokes, ALS (Lou Gehrig's disease), Alzheimer's, and other dementias, and those in permanent vegetative states.

If the patient is in a "terminal condition," he or she may legally have all artificial interventions withdrawn and be permitted to die naturally, with all treatments aimed at maximum comfort and dignity.

Quality of Life

The patient's definition of his or her quality of life should drive the decision making. What does the patient value most? What is he willing to live with or without? Has she ever said what to do in a critical or terminal situation such as this one? If your Mom could sit up in the bed, look you in the eye and say "Do *this!*" what would that be? What is the most loving thing to do in this situation?

The ethical question to answer is: "Can we restore this patient to any semblance of quality of life that would be acceptable to the patient?" This may or may not be the quality of life that is acceptable to the family or caregiver or physician or hospital, but the definition must be tempered and informed by the desires of the patient. This is why advance directives that offer guidance in this area are so important.

Can we restore enough interpersonal interaction so that the stroke or AIDS patient will have a life worth living, despite the other disabilities? If not, we must ask why we are providing treatment that is, by the patient's definition, non-beneficial? Why aren't we changing the goal to comfort only and allowing the patient to die a good death? On whose behalf are we acting?

Or, can we restore the patient to the quality of life that was previously acceptable before this hospitalization occurred? Can the stroke or Alzheimer's patient with the broken hip be restored to the life she was living in the nursing home before she fell? Or will we return her there at a lower level of function that would not be acceptable to her? If the latter, we again must ask why and for whom? Do we honor the patient's life by dishonoring her definition of quality just to assuage our own worries about allowing her to die? Why don't we worry about forcing her to exist in a condition intolerable to her?

If the patient has never stated what his quality of life wishes are, the family can talk together about what they think he would want, based on how he lived. The issue is honoring the life of the patient as he dies. How do we honor his life as we gather around at his death? How do we sustain as much of his quality of life standard as possible as he dies?

Code Status
Every patient in a hospital, nursing home, skilled care facil-

ity, or who is receiving home care has a "resuscitative code status." This designation tells the staff what to do if the patient starts to die. Most places have two categories: 1) Code, 2) No Code. If there is no decision made upon admission, the patient is automatically a *Code* or *Full Code*, or *Category I*, on the presumption that, for most hospitalizations, the patient would want to be resuscitated. If the patient starts to die, or is found not breathing, the caregiver calls a *Code Blue, Dr. Leo,* or some other designation and the "crash team" arrives with a cart full of drugs and implements to attempt full resuscitative measures.

Again, because of media stereotypes and lack of familiarity with the issue, most people have no clue about what happens during a code. The television programs, where nearly every patient given CPR survives, lead families to believe there is a high rate of success with the procedure. People think CPR is benign, expected, standard medical practice for emergency situations, and should therefore always be done.

In fact, the survival to discharge rate for CPR has plummeted in the last twenty-five years to less than three percent because we are using it on broad groups of people for whom it is clearly non-beneficial or futile treatment. The success (survival) rate for CPR for cardiac arrest in nursing homes is even worse: less than one half of one percent, leading some people to argue that the presumption in those facilities ought to be in favor of *not* resuscitating unless requested in a directive.

But CPR is only the beginning, and families need to know what they're buying when they order a Full Code on their loved one. If the patient is elderly or frail (at any age), the process of CPR (hard chest compressions) is likely to crack ribs and possibly puncture lungs. Following the initiation of CPR, the patient will be intubated: a hard plastic tube stuck down the throat into the trachea, bagged by hand, or put on a ventilator (artificial breathing machine), and whisked out of the room to ICU where he or she will be isolated from the family by prison-like visiting hours. That's a Full Code. And it may be exactly what the patient wants, or what the family wants. Some hospitals invite the family to *watch* the code in progress so they can see what is being done to the loved one and evaluate the process for themselves.

Some institutions offer an in-between category, a Category II, or Intermediate Code. This is an excellent option because it gives the patient/family more choice while giving the physician more of a window of opportunity to nudge the patient through this episode, if possible. With this designation, nothing need be withdrawn. All treatments are continued, all medicines given, everything stays the same to try to get the patient through this bout with pneumonia, COPD, stroke, cancer downturn, or kidney failure. But if the treatments are ineffective and the body cannot respond to them and starts to die, the appropriate response is to keep the patient comfortable as the death occurs. No heroic measures are initiated. No CPR is started. No crash cart team appears with high drama and higher expense. A Category II is the best of both worlds for patients in terminal conditions. It allows complete treatment to continue, but saves the patient the indignity, pain, and further suffering of undergoing another futile insult at the end of life.

In most facilities, Category III is called No Code. The phrase itself terrifies people. In fact, as I will suggest later, what we *call* something can sway people toward one decision or the other. People hear only the *No* in the *No Code*. They think the physician and therefore the nurses have given up on the loved one, that they have stopped treatment and will abandon care of their friend or relative.

The truth is we never stop treatment. We change the goal of treatment from cure to palliation (pain control), from aggressive measures to comfort measures, which is why some hospitals are calling their Category III Comfort Category or Comfort Code. This conveys to families what we're going to do, what the appropriate goal is in this terminal situation, and opens the door to a discussion of what comfort really means.

Comfort Care Units

Some institutions are developing Comfort Care Units, or at least protocols that can be helpful in designating the treatment for those needing good comfort care as they die. Other places have Comfort Care procedures that take effect when someone is designated a Category III. The goal of comfort is *comfort*, but the healthcare system is so used to doing things to people (procedures, medicines, tests), that we have forgotten to evaluate these things in the case of terminal patients. Caregivers, then, must diligently guard the comfort of their dying loved ones and question any procedure that is not entirely geared toward the dying patient's comfort. Questions of concern might include:

• Why are we doing lab work on these patients, sticking them with needles to obtain samples that will be used for what?

• Why are we doing blood sugar readings on them? We want to prevent insulin coma as they die? Make sure their blood sugar is normal when they're dead?

• Why are they on monitored units? So we can watch them flat line on the monitor? (You can be dead without a flat line, contrary to TV and movies.)

• Why are we weighing them at four in the morning? Do we really need daily weights on dying people?

• Why are we turning them every two hours? People with bone cancer, for example, get comfortable in the bed in one position only to be rearranged by the nurse to prevent decubitus ulcers (bedsores). If the person will be dead in a few days, why not do what is most comfortable for him or her?

Fairness demands that we understand that these things are not done purposefully to impose further suffering on dying patients, but they are done because we (families and practitioners) are in the middle of a learning curve. We have not yet had enough experience to realize that we don't need to be doing all we previously thought we had to do with dying patients. We can do a lot less with much better results.

The other thing to keep in mind when dealing with loved ones is the difference between "effect" and "benefit." A lot of things are done in medicine and nursing to have an *effect* on the patient's body, on blood pressure, heart rate, kidney output. The question, particularly in patients in a terminal condition, is whether the treatment or medicine or procedure has any *benefit* to that patient.

- Why are we giving antibiotics to Category III patients?
- Why are they getting artificial nutrition/hydration?
- Why are they in ICU/ICN?
- Why are they on cardiac meds, vasopressors, continued chemotherapy, insulin?

When assessing appropriate treatment in terminal patients, families need to ask about the potential benefit, if any, of proposed treatments or procedures, and how they support the goal of comfort.

Food and Water

Just as "life support" is an improper and presumptuous designation until we know the patient's definition of "life," so "food and water" are obfuscating misnomers. The clear plastic object connecting the plastic bag and the blue box with the tube in the patient's nose or stomach is not a feeding tube.

When caregivers use words like "food" and "water," families think "dinner." And, more than that, they think and feel "nurture," "caring," "love." We have incredibly powerful emotional associations with "food and water." We think of feeding helpless babies or old people who can no longer feed themselves. We think of feeding the hungry, of Jesus' admonition to us to feed those less fortunate than ourselves. We feel immediately protective and think that food is a basic human right that must be provided even to those who are in terminal conditions. And we think that, if we withdraw or withhold "food and water" from our dying loved one, he or she will "starve to death."

The truth is that it is not "food and water." The truth is that it is not a "feeding tube." The truth is that nobody "starves to death." The truth is that when we demand that terminal patients receive artificial nutrition/hydration, we often cause more harm than good, the result of which is a "bad death" or certainly a worse one than the person would have had otherwise.

Food and water are things that are taken orally, by mouth, and swallowed. They produce pleasant sensations on the palate and connect with fond memories of meals past. They may alter the patient's mood or attitude, or be the one thing that makes him or her feel normal for a few moments, or provide the joy of sharing a meal with loved ones and friends. One patient, as she was wheeled out of her radiation treatment feeling like hell and having just barfed up her toenails, overheard her friends in the waiting room planning to go out for Mexican food. "I'm going too," she said. And they took her. Another patient with a tube down his nose that constantly sucked out the contents of his stomach asked for his favorite beer. "It'll just come right back out your nose," the always practical staff said. "Yeah," he replied, "but it'll feel so good going down."

Why do dying patients have food restrictions, or why does it take an act of Congress to get a beer or a drink in a hospital room? What's it going to do, kill the person? In this instance, we're kinder to condemned prisoners on Death Row than we are to dying patients.

Again, food and water are ingested by mouth. The stuff in the plastic bag is artificial hydration and artificial nutrition being force-pumped by a machine into a body to keep a body functioning (not necessarily "alive.") It does not come from the dietary department or cafeteria or food service. It comes from the *pharmacy*. If you think it's food, try it. It does not provide the patient any satisfaction or comfort or pleasant memories. It does not alter mood or make the patient feel normal.

But if no one starves to death, what happens when we remove artificial nutrition and hydration from patients in a terminal condition? Azotemia happens.

The Role of Azotemia

In the normal process of dying, patients quit eating and drinking. This is extremely important to remember when dealing with nursing home patients. One study looked at such patients who were walking and talking one week and dead three weeks later, because they had quit eating and drinking for no apparent reason. They were not hungry or thirsty, refused all entreaties from staff and families to ingest (so the staff and families would feel better), became azotemic, and died. It was as though they woke up one morning and a chromosome timer in their brain clicked, indicating it was time to go. Often, families, nursing administrators, physicians (worried about lawyers), and uninformed caregivers will not let this natural process occur. Instead, when someone quits eating in a nursing home, she is rushed off to a local emergency room to have a percutaneous enterostomal gastrostomy tube (PEG) inserted surgically to force artificial nutrition and hydration (AN/H) into her and prolong her death as long as technically possible.

When we withdraw AN/H from patients in terminal conditions, azotemia begins. They do not experience hunger or thirst, though they might like their mouths moistened with swabs or ice chips. The patient begins to dehydrate and expel fluids. For patients with brain swelling, this process sometimes results in temporary clarity because the edema (fluid) drains and decreases the pressure on brain tissue. As dehydration occurs, waste products build up in the body and serve as a natural analgesic to insulate the body from pain.

The patient becomes tired, sleepy, less and less conscious, drops into a coma where all pain ceases, and eventually dies. This process can take from a few days to a few weeks, depending on the debility of the body and the advance of disease. If there is any pain or discomfort from the disease during this time, it can be quelled with the large range of pharmaceuticals available from aspirin to morphine, and the many routes of administration, from sublingual to i.v., to patch, to suppository. Indeed, azotemia results in a good death.

So what happens if we maintain AN/H in the patient in a terminal condition? Studies show we create a bad death. As we pump nutrition and fluids into the body that is trying to throw them off and die, we create what are called "clinical sequelae," things that happen as a result of our treatments— that do not happen with azotemia. The constant influx of fluids means that the patient will have to be catheterized and suctioned. As kidneys shut down and fluid keeps coming in, those fluids begin to seep into bloating tissues. This condition is very painful and requires increased narcotic medication. Artificial nutrition can result in intractable (unstoppable) diarrhea, and it can wake up the patient so he or she can fully (and unnecessarily) experience suffering and death.

What To Do?

We do these things not because we are bad healthcare practitioners or stupid family members, but because we are in that learning curve regarding the technical imperative. We haven't yet learned that we not only do not have to do all these things to persons in terminal conditions, but also that to do "everything possible" results in a bad death with unnecessary prolongation of suffering.

The difficulty is in knowing when we cross the line from sustaining the quality of life acceptable to the patient, and prolonging dying. Part of the problem lies in the language with which we discuss these issues, because our biomedical technology has outpaced our descriptive vocabulary. We don't have good words to describe what it is that we're actually doing or the machinery/techniques we're using, so we fall back on convenient, traditional descriptors or medical slang that inaccurately frame the discussion. "Life support," "food and water," "feeding tube," all come with vast amounts of emotional baggage that get in the way of seeing the situation accurately, and they result in treatment decisions that cause harm, prolong dying, and do not honor the wishes of the patient.

Another key issue is the previously mentioned difference between "effect" and "benefit." Most of what is done in medicine is aimed at having an effect on the body, organ, or system. But for patients in terminal conditions, the question is not whether you can produce an effect with the antibiotic or I.V. or ventilator or AN/H, the question is whether or not this treatment or procedure results in any benefit to the patient at all (as the patient would define benefit). If not, comfort care is in order.

Many people worry about removing treatment of any kind for fear of causing the death of the loved one and feeling as though they have committed murder. It is extremely important to understand the truth about this. When a ventilator is turned off, the cause of death is not turning off the ventilator. The cause of death is pulmonary failure, which was happening before the ventilator was turned on in the first place. When AN/H are removed the cause of death is not starvation or dehydration. The cause of death is the underlying disease process, cancer or heart disease or trauma or whatever. Withdrawing treatment is merely getting out of the way and allowing the natural process of death to occur with as much attention to comfort, dignity, and quality as possible. It is often the most loving (and difficult) thing to do both to honor the wishes of the patient and to come to terms with the inevitability of the death.

Home or Hospital?

A number of years ago, a study was done to ask hospice patients where they wanted to die. Almost unanimously they said that they wanted to die at home. Then their caretakers and family were asked where they wanted the patient to die. Almost unanimously they responded that they wanted the loved one to die in the hospital. Often the patient's definition of "a good death" includes final moments in familiar surroundings, with family and friends and animals around, looking at or being in the midst of pictures, furniture, sights and sounds that are well known and comforting.

But the family or caregivers are often afraid that they will not be able to take care of the person adequately at home. The thought of bathing or changing or cleaning up a parent or grandparent may be awkward or embarrassing; or there may be a fear of not controlling pain or not knowing what to do when death occurs. Thus the family can feel more at ease in a hospital or nursing home where others are paid to handle bodily and medication needs and where they are likely to be guided by experienced professionals at the time of death.

The choice is dependent on many variables. Does insurance cover home care or terminal inpatient care? Many insurers are now underwriting hospice care because it is much less costly in the last months of life. What is the home situation and is there enough time to train caregivers adequately and support them so that they can provide the needed care comfortably and reliably? Most importantly, what are the wishes of the dying patient? Once again, it is necessary to raise the issue of what a good death means to the person early enough in the process so that such plans can be made.

If the patient is in a hospital, nursing home, rehab hospital, or skilled facility, families need to know that there are always people around to help with decisions and information. Most facilities have a chaplain, social worker, case manager, or patient representative who can be paged by the nurse or the switchboard operator. These people will meet with them in the patient's room or in another convenient place. They need not be Lone Rangers in determining the right thing to do. An objective third party can advise them of their options and tell them what others have done in these situations to help them come to the best decision for themselves and the patient.

As stated at the opening of this book, a major educational issue is that we have forgotten how people die and the popular media (not to mention our "educational" institutions) are remiss in teaching us even now. But with proper instruction and support from other caregivers, such as home health and hospice, families can honor the wish of the patient to spend his or her last days at home, without being dragged off by EMS to an emergency room or ICU to suffer further indignities. Likewise, families can be present at the bedside in nursing homes, where many patients will want to spend their last hours because that's where they have spent their last months or years and it is now more familiar than home. The point is to honor the patient's wish for a good death in the surroundings of his or her choice.

Ethics Committees

Nearly every hospital has an ethics committee and most nursing facilities either have one or can access the nearby hospital committee. If patients or caregivers are confused about what to do, which treatment to withdraw, whether to continue treatment at all, what outcomes are likely, or simply what the "right thing" is, they can ask for an ethics consult.

Ethics committees are comprised of people, mostly from the community (not just the facility), who are interested in ethical issues and have some expertise in this area. Members typically include a chaplain or other clergy, social worker, nurse, physician, attorney, educator, consumer, layperson with no involvement in healthcare, and often a psychologist. Many facilities have a smaller Ethics Consult Group which can be called on short notice to screen or make an initial assessment of the issue and, if necessary, convene the larger committee. Seldom is this required. In fact, most issues can be discussed with the committee leader at the bedside with the patient (if capable), family, and physician. Consensus of the committee is not binding; it serves a consultative function and offers an opinion of what the ethical choices might be in the situation. The committee might offer suggestions for further deliberation or refer to resources that others have not considered. In any case, it can be a valuable source of feedback and support.

The Role of Hospice

An obvious option, but one that is often not chosen until the very last few days of life, is hospice. Nearly every community in the country now has hospice services available and almost all insurance companies provide coverage for it. Hospice has taught the healthcare field everything we know about pain management. It is what they do best. With hospice on board patients can go home with excellent comfort care provided by the hospice home health agency under the supervision of a medical director who is skilled in quelling the problems of terminal patients.

Though most places offer hospice as a home health option, some communities have an inpatient hospice where patients who do not want to die in a facility or home can be transferred. Other places offer licensed "hospice beds" in the hospital or skilled nursing setting. Hospice can attend to the person whether at home, in the hospital, or in a nursing home. In fact, patients in nursing homes often get better care when under the supervision of hospice. And, because they are seen as a "known death," both by anxious staff and nervous administrators, they are less likely to be mistakenly resuscitated and transferred to a hospital at the last minute. If your community does not have a hospice program of any kind, check with the local hospital or clinic to find out which home health agency does the best terminal care.

Hospice not only takes care of the patient, they educate and support the family in this difficult time. They also do follow-up bereavement care to answer questions and deal with the many issues around grieving. It can be an excellent avenue for providing a good death.

Let me say this once more with feeling: the appropriate treatment goal for patients in a terminal condition is *comfort*. Everything should be aimed at meeting the patient's definition of comfort, dignity, safety, and quality. Honor the patient's life as death approaches. A good death is one that is consistent with the life that preceded it.

For a more detailed review of the specific issues noted here, see my book *Surviving Death: A Practical Guide to Caring for the Dying and the Bereaved.* Chapters include: How to Be with Dying Patients; Pulling the Plug. How Do We Decide?; Death and Spirituality; Sex After Death; Surviving Death, Grief Tasks.

Many hospice and medical training programs have used this book as a resource. It is the distillation of my twenty years in healthcare at the bedside of dying patients, dealing with their grieving families, and is available either through Twenty-Third Publications (P.O. Box 180, Mystic, CT 06355), or your local bookstore.

This chapter has dealt with how we die and the options available for a good death, given the healthcare system with which we have to negotiate. Through all of this, patients, families, and caregivers must be assertive and persistent, not because providers are bad or family members are ignorant, but because we have not yet, as a culture, learned how to give good deathcare. It is only with caring persistence that the system will gradually change, one patient at a time, one physician at a time, as we gain more experience with the possibility that a good death is not an oxymoron.

3

ALTERNATIVES TO TRADITIONAL TREATMENT

This is not a New Age chapter about alternatives to dying, such as transcending, transitioning, or metamorphosing. It is about alternatives to traditional treatment at the end of life. But first it is necessary to put some basic assumptions out on the table.

The difference between "traditional" and "alternative" may depend on where you were brought up. If you live in the Southwest you may be partial to *curanderos*, healers with generations of knowledge of natural medicine and rituals. Native Americans have a powerful tradition of tribal medicine, while Asians may rely on various foods and desiccated herbs. Physical manipulation, massage, cultural remedies (often prepared by designated people within that tradition), uses of heat, cold, chants, prayers, religious objects, and laying on of hands are all thought to be efficacious. To a friend of mine, raised in a Czech community in the Texas Valley, alternative medicine was what the doctors practiced compared with the traditional folk remedies of his family.

For purposes of discussion here, "traditional" means the allopathic model of medicine practiced predominantly in this country since the early 1900s. This interpretation can reflect a highly prejudicial cultural bias and is not meant to imply that traditional is good or effective and anything else is bad or ineffective. Often the opposite is true.

"Alternative" medicine, until recently, was considered by the medical community as something akin to voodoo (which, by the way, also works for some people). With the increasing demands on a medical system unable to cope with the influx of aging people and uninsured people, many Americans are going outside the system. In recent years, studies show that Americans are paying more visits to alternative practitioners than to traditional ones. They are spending billions of dollars on alternative treatment that is accessible, user friendly, and often produces results without the side effects, hassle, or paternalistic attitudes of traditional medicine (not to mention the lesser cost).

The truth is that lots of things work. Traditional and alternative medicine both have treatments, procedures, remedies, and methodologies that make sense and have proven outcomes. Both do a lot of things that are useless and wasteful, and both are sometimes dispensed by paternalistic egomaniacs. Yet, it is still important to know something about all possible options.

There are studies going on all over the country today, combining traditional and alternative (now referred to in the more positive light of "complementary") medicines. Cardiac bypass patients in a New York hospital are undergoing relaxation, hypnosis, healing touch, and acupuncture before, during, and after the operation. Predicted results include quicker initial recovery from anesthesia and surgery, faster healing, and more satisfied customers. The lesson here for patients and families is not to abandon the care of your doctor in favor of shamans, but to combine the best of both worlds in support of the goal of the patient to have a good death. Here are possible options.

Hospice: We've already mentioned this one, but it still needs to be at the top of the list. It is the best alternative in the system, though it is incredible how few physicians will refer people to it, or think of it for their patients, until the last few days. It should be considered much earlier in the course of terminal illness as a means of aiming for a good death.

Home Care: This alternative can be handled with home health services and lots of family and community support. In addition to the usual advance directives (Living Will, Durable Power of Attorney for Healthcare), some states now have an Out Of Hospital Do Not Resuscitate Order. Patients who do not wish to be resuscitated by EMS or transferred to an emergency room can, along with their physician, fill out this form (or have it filled out by their surrogate). The form is kept with the chart and the patient receives a wrist band stating "OHDNR," so that if someone inadvertently or in a panic calls EMS, the responders check the wristband or form and do not have to start CPR or transfer to a hospital. It is another way to honor the rights and the desires of the patient.

Complementary Medicine

Unfortunately, this covers everything from chiropractic to crystals. Because most of these treatments are unregulated, there may be a greater chance of quackery or rip-offs, so choose products and practitioners carefully. You may be able to get a referral from your physician, or from a friend who has had success with a particular person or treatment. While this is not meant to be a compendium of offerings, a quick look at the options may be helpful.

Chiropractic: Probably the most mainstream of treatment alternatives, chiropractors are usually covered by insurance. Traditional clinicians and physician clinics have even hired them as an adjunct to their practices, or affiliated with them in some manner. Chiropractors may be able to assist with pain relief through manipulation, massage, or muscle exercises.

Acupuncture: Practiced for over 5000 years, if any treatment is "traditional," it is this one. Based on strengthening the "chi" in a system of energy meridians that span the body, it may be particularly useful for addressing pain and discomfort issues, including anxiety and stress relief (for family members as well as patients). Tiny needles are inserted into the skin to effect the energy flow on the meridians. Because the needles only penetrate the outer layer of skin, they do not hurt the patient. Sometimes a very small amount of electric current is attached to the needles to increase their effectiveness. Often acupuncture practitioners are knowledgeable about Chinese and other herbal mixtures that may help as well. Several states now license acupuncturists, permit them to practice in hospitals, and reimburse them with insurance.

Homeopathy: The predominant medical model in the U.S. in the nineteenth century (and still widely practiced in Europe), homeopathy uses infinitesimal doses of natural substances to treat "like with like." The theory is that a small dose of a substance that causes an illness can cure it, not unlike vaccinations. Naturopathy is a close cousin in its use of natural substances, though not in infinitesimal doses.

Aruveydic: Based on ancient (10,000 year old) Hindu aruveydic scriptures, this system of addressing illness and death is the epitome of mind/body interaction. Deep breathing, relaxation, guided imagery, diet, exercise, spiritual purification, and sometimes acupuncture and herbs, are all a part of this method. The contemporary author Deepak Chopra is one of its most popular proponents.

Healing Touch: This involves moving the hands over the patient to "absorb" the pain or negative energy and smooth out the rough or uneven energy spots. It is totally non-invasive and the patient is a passive recipient of the practitioner's offering. A corollary to this is the more traditional (in religious circles) "laying on of hands" and anointing with blessed oil, frequently done by clergy. Another corollary is, of course, therapeutic massage. Patients often relax incredibly well following back, foot, hand, or head massage.

Herbs: Herbologists have written volumes on the therapeutic effects of these natural substances, which have been known to be highly efficacious for centuries. Some well established health-food stores have knowledgeable people in the herb/vitamin section. The important point to remember here is to make sure there is no detrimental combination of herbs and prescription medications.

Crystals, Aromas: Crystals are at least benign and at most helpful in some way. Clearly they are the least invasive alternative of all, as they just hang there, hopefully conducting positive energies. Aroma therapy produces pleasing scents that are supposed to have therapeutic value. Some are rubbed into different parts of the body. Some are simply inhaled or put in a room to affect the atmosphere. Again, assuming the patient has positive associations with the smells, they are at least comforting. Tom Robbins, author of *Jitterbug Perfume*, would argue that the olfactory sense is the most developed and important one of all.

Meditation: Included under this "alternative" are yoga, hypnotherapy, guided imagery, relaxation techniques, therapeutic massage, and reflexology. All of these things add to the comfort of the patient (and of caregivers) by relaxing muscle groups and providing soothing sounds or even silence, away from the usual bright lights and intrusive demands often experienced by those undergoing medical care.

Other environmental concerns include music that is comforting or fun for the patient, pictures (including photographs, videos, or paintings), favorite foods, special people or animals (even stuffed ones), hydrotherapy (swimming or jacuzzi), or going on special outings as available. All of these alternatives may add to the comfort and pleasure of the patient and family.

General Suggestions

Remember, a lot of things work. Remember too, that "work" means something is beneficial to the patient, not necessarily having an obvious effect on his or her condition or system. But also remember to use your common sense and stay focused on the goal, which is healing, not cure. Lots of things can be healed. Memories can be healed. Dreams can be healed. Angers, guilts, resentments of a lifetime can be healed. Family relationships can be healed. And all of this healing can take place in the course of terminal illness and dying. In this context it is important to remember that death and healing are not opposites, and that death is often a form of healing. With this in mind, alternatives to "traditional" treatment can be chosen for their therapeutic value, that is, their value to enhancing the quality of life of the patient as death approaches.

Be careful not to choose alternative or complementary providers out of the phone book or from a New Age newspaper. There are a lot of quacks out there looking to make a fast buck off of emotionally vulnerable family members. Just as with traditional practitioners, quacks range from benign con artists to delusional zealots who can hasten someone's death through their incompetence or inexperience. Instead, find people by referral from others who have used such providers with success and satisfaction. Confer with your physician, nurses, physical therapists, chaplains, social workers, or the patient representative, for a referral to a reputable resource. Go to the local health food store and ask at the vitamin/herb counter for reliable people. Be sure to share with others what happened and how well you were served.

Beware of people who tell you with overwhelming

confidence that they can "help," or even worse, "cure" your loved one, especially if their assistance involves a lot of money or time. Your job is to provide comfort for the patient and yourself, not to waste time and resources doing more things than even traditional medicine would prescribe.

Tell your doctor if you are using any treatment that is at all invasive or could interact with the medication being used. The worst thing that can happen is that the physician will ridicule you for using unorthodox methods or ask if you are questioning his or her ability to treat your loved one. Most enlightened physicians will understand that many things work in different ways and will not feel defensive about working in tandem with alternative/complementary treatments. At the least they may consider the modalities benign. In any case, just make sure that the herb you are providing doesn't counteract medication or become toxic when combined with the drugs your loved one is taking. The primary rule of thumb, just as for your physician, is to "do no harm."

Many people find alternative ways to enhance the quality of the final days of life for their loved ones. Others do just fine with more traditional care. In either case, it is important to know options and how to choose them for the best death possible for our loved ones, and ultimately for ourselves.

The ultimate "alternative" treatment is to hasten someone's death by euthanasia, a subject so important it requires its own chapter.

4

Euthanasia

The word euthanasia comes from two Greek words (*euthanatos*) meaning "a good death." It does not intrinsically imply actually killing someone. In its fullest sense, it means providing the opportunity for a good death, however that may come about. It is a prominent issue for us now because, as already mentioned, the aging Baby Boomers are interacting with the healthcare system in droves and they are seeing first-hand the current national requirement of high-tech death. They are watching the way their parents, grandparents, and friends (and each other) are experiencing the remnants of the technological imperative, dying in intensive care units on ventilators, or in nursing homes wasting away to shreds of their former selves, and they don't like what they see.

Many among them have disliked and rebelled against authority for fifty years and see the medical system and those who work in it as just one more example of ridiculously anachronistic, restrictive rules they need to break. When facing death these people want to do it their way, with no restrictions and the right to hasten the inevitable when and how they want. Many argue that there may be a place for this alternative in certain circumstances; others argue that there is not.

Those Who Oppose It
Opponents of euthanasia argue that such requests are a sign of hopelessness, depression, the devaluing of life itself. They

believe that if these emotional concerns were addressed effectively, people would not want to die. The issue is a psychological one and should be managed with psychotropic medication and therapy, because no one in his or her "right mind" would want to hasten death. In addition, there is the potential uncertainty of outcome as well as the possibility of mis-diagnosis. Many people who were given up as hopeless cases are alive today. Others were mis-diagnosed with terminal illness and would have made a horrible mistake by taking their own lives.

Furthermore, opponents argue, it is selfish to want to die and take your life into your own hands. Patients should think of the effect that actively causing their death will have on family and friends who may be left with decades of guilt or resentment, unresolved until their own death.

Finally, many opponents believe that such a method is sacrilegious. It usurps the power of a sovereign God who has a plan for every person's life, a plan that is thwarted at the person's spiritual peril.

Those Who Support It

Proponents argue that euthanasia is just one more way to assert control in a situation (dying) where everything else is out of control. They believe that it is the ultimate patient right to refuse treatment and the final right to choose the preferred kind of death as opposed to succumbing to the inevitable over-treatment so predominant in healthcare institutions. They argue that it provides the patients with a choice for a timely death, largely under their own control, rather than at the behest of someone else.

Furthermore, they argue, hastening the death maintains the dignity of the person, who will not have to await the gradual wasting of the body as friends and family stand by, taking over embarrassing personal care needs as the patient weakens and drops into a coma.

Serious proponents of assistance have even argued for an advance directive for assistance in dying (like a Living Will), because they believe such a document might actually prolong life rather than hasten death. Patients diagnosed with ALS, Alzheimer's, stroke, PVS, or other conditions with a known terminal trajectory, could sign such a directive designating the conditions of too much suffering (including but not limited to pain issues). When all of those conditions are reached, a designated caregiver would be legally empowered to assist them with dying—so that they would not choose to die before that time or suffering came.

To support their assertion, proponents cite the case of the first woman who went to Jack Kevorkian. Janet Adkins was diagnosed in her mid-fifties with early Alzheimer's. She was already seeing deficits and knew that when she got further down the disease and suffering trajectory, no one could legally help her to die. So she went to Michigan to cause her own death while she was still in control.

An advance directive for assistance in dying when her suffering became intractable would likely have obviated the need she felt to choose death so early in the process, thereby depriving herself, her family, and her community of at least months, possibly even years, of relatively high quality of life. Such proponents argue that a directive would have extended both the quantity and quality of her life.

Money and Healthcare
Interestingly enough, people on all sides of the assistance in dying debate are generally agreed that it should not be a legal option until we have some form of universal access to healthcare, because money becomes an issue. They concur that

euthanasia or assistance may look like a more reasonable route to the forty-two million Americans with no health insurance anyway, who will get fewer tests in the emergency room and die in greater numbers there than people with insurance.

Furthermore, not only are the uninsured at risk, but so are elderly persons who may choose assistance in dying far too early simply to avoid depleting their lifetime savings on the last few months of life rather than providing it for their families. Nearly everyone agrees that money must be removed from the equation.

The role of the physician remains a controversial one. One side argues that they are the only ones capable of successfully prescribing the correct amount of drugs and that assistance in dying is the physician's obligation on the long continuum of care from birth to death. Others counter that such a practice would negate the physician/patient contract based on trust.

Finally, proponents argue that euthanasia values quality of life over quantity of life. Many people want to live until they are no longer conscious, or until they can no longer care for themselves, or they may wish to die before ever reaching those conditions. They believe that the quality of their lives matters more than life itself. They believe in having the right to end their existence before they are condemned to slow, biological destruction from disease, injury, or illness.

Some proponents respond to the charge that "assistance in dying is sacrilegious" by asserting that it in fact shows confidence in God's mercy and a strong belief in an afterlife. They argue that society is consistently kinder to our animals, which we put to sleep rather than let suffer debility and disease, while we demand that humans suffer the final indignities of their terminal conditions.

Obviating the Need

In fact, it generally ought to be possible to obviate the *need* for assistance in dying, so that it is not necessary to use euthanasia as an end-run around a system that requires high-tech dying. To prepare ourselves and others, we need to consider the following guidelines.

Tell the truth. We need honesty at initial diagnosis. Families must press for information about known outcomes of treatments. Healthcare providers must educate families and patients of *all* their options, including the choice of comfort care and transfer to home or hospice. We need to tell the truth about treatments, their toxicity, and their effect on the quality of life in the final months of the patient with a terminal condition. Often truth-telling will allow patients and families to make choices early on that provide comfort and so weigh against the patient ending up in a situation where they perceive that the only way out is assistance in dying.

Equally value comfort and high-tech. The presumption of the medical community is still in favor of aggressive treatment, even in the face of death. People who choose comfort, hospice, or home care with family, are often denigrated or seen as quitting, giving up, not fighting with everything possible for as long as their bodies will stand the assault. If we equally value comfort care, and offer it as just one more treatment modality, people might choose it earlier. They might refuse treatments or technology that prolong the inevitable or get them through the event that would have caused their death, only to get them well enough to linger indefinitely.

Better pain management. As a medical system, we are abysmal at pain control. A Robert Wood Johnson Foundation study of nine thousand dying patients showed that over fifty percent of them died in moderate to severe pain. Because we have confused narcotics with "drugs," we often refuse to give narcotics to patients who are dying. ("Don't give my dying 80-year-old mother morphine for pain. She'll get addicted!" As if she would live long enough to become addicted.) But the truth is, once patients get their pain under control, they want to die a lot less. Patients or families who request assistance in dying ought to be fully evaluated for pain management to be sure that issue is resolved to the satisfaction of the patient. If we resolved pain issues and were unafraid of providing narcotic and other pain remedies, regardless of their alleged sedative effect, there would likely be less desire for assistance in death.

Do not judge others who are in pain. Even after we do everything possible to offer alternatives and to alleviate pain and quell suffering, there still will be patients who believe that the only relief from suffering is death. These patients, who are often in *intractable* (unrelievable) suffering, might well choose the option of assistance if it does not jeopardize those who help and care for them.

Again, the important thing to remember with this issue is that everything possible should be done to obviate the need a person might feel for assistance in dying. Even when assistance is seen by a patient as a reasonable action of last resort in the case of intractable suffering, the best method of accomplishing it is still to *discontinue* artificial interventions, from artificial nutrition and hydration to antibiotics and insulin. Doing this is not really assisting, it is withdrawing futile treatment and allowing the natural process of azotemia or uremia and death to occur. It would then only be in extreme cases, where existence is intolerable, that patients would seek assistance in dying. In all of this, family members and caregivers should offer loved ones compassion and understanding, rather than prejudicial judgment.

Most importantly, patients and their caretakers should get an objective opinion or evaluation, especially regarding pain management and withdrawal of nutrition and fluids, before assuming that assistance in dying is the only course of action to take. Hospital or hospice chaplains, ethics committees, social workers, or the local medical society can offer names of reputable people with whom to discuss the issues. Unilateral decisions are almost always unnecessary, and often result in less than optimal care at the end.

Patients often state that the worst thing about dying is the loneliness. That, too, is a comfort issue, and we ought, as noted above, to assure patients that we will stand by them, assisting them however we can to maintain control in a situation where they are more and more dependent. We ought not to abandon them by refusing to honor their wish to attain a good death. Neither should we hasten them toward it out of frustration with or ignorance of the alternatives.

As other states begin to examine, explore, and possibly follow Oregon's lead with the Death with Dignity Act, allowing assistance in dying, much public debate is needed. If our society eventually does come to legal and ethical consensus on this issue, we must make certain that strict and proper boundaries are set and responsibilities are clearly defined in order to minimize the capricious or malicious abuse of assistance in dying.

5

THE ROLE OF SPIRITUALITY

Spirituality is often an issue in a good death, whether or not the person is religious. When diagnosed with a terminal condition or life-threatening illness, patients and their families try to make sense of what is happening and put it into the broader context of understanding their lives. Some people have said that the task of life is coming to terms with our own death. Terminal illness is, presumably, our last shot at doing that.

Unfortunately, dying people quickly learn that everyone has an opinion about what they should do, pray for, think, and believe. Patients report with dismay that friends, family, and visitors are eager to "share" their opinions with or without provocation, though the sharing often comes across as "imposing."

Mentioned previously, the book *Surviving Death* details many of the insensitive, judgmental, "religious" things people say, from "God will cure him/her," to "You don't die 'til your number comes up." It also deals with the theological underpinnings of these statements and others, along with the "death-myths" people use to avoid treatment decisions. Clearly, most of what is thought to be Judeo-Christian theology is in fact American civil religion and is patently unhelpful to people trying to find their spiritual way to a good death.

Contrary to what many dying patients are told by well-meaning visitors, God does not want or purposely plan for people to be sick or dead; only a callous God would do that.

God does not send suffering and tragedy to teach us lessons or draw us closer; only a cruel God would do that. God does not take loved ones away for mysteriously unfathomable reasons, about which we are to remain calmly docile and piously unquestioning; only an egocentric God would do that. God does not capriciously punish us or our loved ones with death; only a vindictive God would do that.

But if God doesn't do these things, what does God do? Many people find it helpful to hear (the Good News) that God does with us exactly what we can do with each other: *be there.* It is God's constant and eternal presence in our lives and in our deaths that is supportively transforming, providing the assurance that "whether we live or die, we are the Lord's." This straightforward message and promise of presence (both God's and ours) is found to be far more helpful than the platitudes in the preceding paragraph.

Struggling with Issues

People seeking a good death often struggle with the issue of whether there is a spiritual duty to live or spiritual permission to die. The duty to live is usually based on the beliefs that: All life is sacred; God is sovereign; Suffering is redemptive; and Death is the enemy. Spiritual permission to die and to actively seek a good death is often based on the beliefs that: All life has meaning; We are co-creators with God; Suffering is unnecessary; and Death is healing.

Our culture seems to infer that, if all life is sacred, then the patient must try every possible medical treatment that could conceivably prolong physical existence. Artificial interventions must never be removed and the person must experience a high-tech death. But in fact this same culture ironically fails to treat all life as sacred. It kills prisoners, and armies, and perpetrators, and allows people with less economic means to go without basic health services, even though this will lessen their longevity.

If, on the other hand, *all life has meaning*, then the patient is the definer of that meaning. It becomes the patient's right to determine what faculties or abilities he or she will live with or without, what level of quality of life has enough meaning to be sustained in it. Often that meaning is stated partly in spiritual terms, the ability to pray or interact with community, the willingness to "go on" to the next "larger life."

Many people assert that to believe *God is sovereign* means to passively submit to what appears to be the capricious will of a vengeful God who afflicts us with unwarranted suffering. For these persons, an all-knowing God plans everything that happens, knows the day they will die, and basically aims them toward that final chapter.

To believe, however, as the apostle Paul did, that we are "co-creators with God" is to take seriously our responsibility to choose and our freedom to act. It is to make us active collaborators in our fate and to do everything we can to position ourselves for a good death, rather than accepting what we get.

People who believe that suffering is necessary claim that pain medication should be kept at a minimum. They believe that opportunities for suffering should be borne with gratitude for the chance to guarantee forgiveness and redemption.

But there is nothing intrinsically redemptive about suffering. Chaplains who work in the nation's prisons report that there is nothing intrinsically "penitential" about incarceration. Some inmates use the time for life review and reflection while others use it to plot more dastardly deeds or learn how to better commit crimes. Likewise, dying people are incarcerated for a death sentence and their responses are the same. Some use the time for reflection and repair of relationships; others become bitter, withdrawn, and frightened. Particularly given our effective pharmacology, it is clear that suffering is unnecessary. It is neither required for redemption nor to fully experience the final moments of death, as one might wish to experience the pain of childbirth.

Finally, people who believe that death is the evil enemy must fight it with all possible help from our medical armamentarium. To do any less would be to give up the battle to the forces of evil in the world who are battling for our bodies and souls. But if, as I have suggested earlier, death can be a form of healing, we would treat our terminally ill patients and their grieving families in a vastly different manner than under current medical practice. The goal of their care would be comfort rather than needlessly subjecting them to futile attempts to prolong their inevitable and often wished-for death.

Spiritual Turn-Arounds

Hospital chaplains are frequently asked if dying people suddenly have spiritual turn-arounds at the last minute, as in the movies. I have never seen this happen. My experience is that people die the way they live. If spirituality was an issue when they were healthy, it remains an issue; if not, it seldom is given much thought as something that suddenly needs attention. People are pretty consistent in their living and dying.

Occasionally, the "incarceration" of illness (just as physical incarceration for prisoners) provides the time and the lucidity to do a life review, so that patients and families may recall things they wish they had done differently. Sometimes they may be motivated to seek reconciliation or at least forgiveness regarding these concerns. Addressing and perhaps resolving unfinished business is a spiritual issue, though it need not be framed in that manner to be discussed or accomplished. Spirituality takes many forms, from religious to secular. It is important for those seeking a good death to have the opportunity to review issues in the areas of reconciliation, forgiveness, healing, and blessing.

Reconciliation: Unfinished business may be a source of discomfort or spiritual pain for the dying person. There may be family members, friends, enemies, people wronged or treated badly, who the patient needs or wants to see before death finishes the business permanently and perhaps unresolved. Likewise, there may be family members or others who want to resolve issues with the dying person. Often the help of a chaplain, clergy, social worker, or trained counselor can facilitate this exchange for the benefit of all parties, and reconciliation can occur. Once reconciled, or, if that is not possible, the attempt made, the patient may approach a better if not a good death with less pain or suffering.

Forgiveness: There are very few of us who do not have people whose forgiveness we want, or people who are in need of our forgiveness. This, in fact, may be the biggest spiritual impediment to a good death with a clear conscience. Whether addressed with clergy, sacraments, counseling, confession to a friend or loved one, followed by affirmation and acceptance, patients often die more peacefully and at ease. Some patients have written letters, left audio or videotapes, or e-mailed messages to initiate this process.

Healing: As mentioned earlier, healing takes place even in the course of dying. Memories, dreams, relationships, angers, guilts, resentments, failures, regrets: all can be healed, often through reconciliation or forgiveness. Sometimes, in the case of comatose or otherwise unresponsive patients, this can be done by the community around the dying person. When the friends lowered the man on the pallet through the roof tiles to Jesus, we are told that "when Jesus saw *their faith,* he was healed." It was not the faith of the sick person, but the faith and love and belief of the people around the sick person that brought about healing.

It is important to remember not to impose our will in any way on sick, dying people. There will be plenty of people and institutions who will gladly do that. At the same time, if we know the unfinished wish of the patient, it can be helpful to offer that at the bedside in the form of prayer or personal intervention. Comatose patients can often hear, so it might be important for them to hear the word of forgiveness or love or reconciliation from a particular person. If that is not possible, the words of acceptance and pardon from a religious tradition might be offered as an assuaging balm against spiritual suffering.

Blessing: This issue is probably the most powerful spiritual activity to offer a dying person. In biblical times, offering one's blessing meant affirming the person regardless of what he or she had done or might do. It meant total unconditional acceptance and encouragement of the other person without thought for what could be offered in return. Dying patients may need to think of ways to bless their children or parents or friends or spouses, in language or means that will make sense to them. It may be through doing or saying something to the person, from writing a letter or poem to actually touching or laying hands on the person's head to confer the blessing. Blessing goes beyond forgiveness and reconciliation, transcends both of those to convey to the other person a sense of thankfulness and appreciation. It is a very powerful thing to be given and received.

Sometimes dying patients need or want the blessing of someone to alleviate their suffering or to validate their efforts toward that person over the years. Often this is the case with parents and children. Maybe the last best thing we can give to our loved ones as parents or children is our blessing of them.

It may be the final gift for a good death.

In all of these issues there needs to be a quick word said about prayer; two words, actually: method and purpose.

Method: The method that most respects patients is three-fold: ask, ask, ask.

•Ask if the person wants to pray. Contrary to popular belief, people don't need anyone praying for them and can do it themselves. There are many kinds of prayer, and they may be practicing the method that makes the most sense to them without demanding it be done in a certain "religious" manner or with proscribed words or phrases.

•If the person does want to pray, ask this second question: What do you want to pray about? It is impossible and unrealistic, not to mention coercive, to assume that we know what people want to pray about. Jesus didn't assume. When the blind man came up to him, rather than reaching for the man's eyes, he asked: "What is it you want?" When we do this, we must pay close attention, because people will tell us, and we may have to repeat it back in a prayer.

•Ask again. "Do you want to start or do you want me to start?" Some people will start eagerly, but others will want you to start. Still others won't believe it's a prayer unless you read it from a book. The point here is to give people a chance to put their words into prayer themselves if they are able, according to their own tradition. It is also a way to continue to empower them in a situation where they are likely experiencing less and less control because of their illness.

Purpose: This is crucial. Patients will have a bad death if visitors utter desperate prayers for miraculous cures over their dying bodies. Dying persons can feel sad or even angry that they cannot meet the wish of the loved one, or dismayed that they have been spiritually abandoned at the end. Therefore, it is extremely important to remember that the purpose of prayer is *presence* not *outcome*. If prayer is appropriate, the appropriate prayer is for the presence of the Holy in this situation, to be present with the patient and everyone else with that patient, regardless of outcome. It is the presence of the divine that is empowering, assuaging, supporting, reconciling, forgiving, loving. And it is that presence that invokes or inspires others to be present with the patient wherever their life trajectory goes.

Spirituality is highly individualized, perhaps like souls. It is an area of the utmost vulnerability and deepest intimacy and must be handled with great care and much respect. It can also be a powerful area of closure and relief, the unburdening of issues or feelings that can block or preclude a good death.

6

How to Get a Good Death

The only way to assure that you or your loved one will achieve a good death in the current healthcare environment is to begin talking about it today, planning for it now. As you read this last chapter, jot down the things you have not discussed or taken care of for yourself or the patient. Then set a time to accomplish them.

Quality of Life

The most important issue to discuss with the person who will be making your healthcare and treatment decisions is your own definition of quality of life. The discussion need not be definitive; you can't think of every possible situation and determine your response to it. That's impossible. Instead, consider some of these common scenarios and offer guidelines if they should occur.

Stroke: What cognitive and physical functions are you willing to live with or without? What do you think you would want done if you lost the ability to communicate? If you could respond with eye blinks? If you could not swallow food or water and had to be kept alive with a PEG surgically inserted in your abdomen to provide artificial nutrition and artificial hydration?

Dementia: If, as a result of stroke, disease, or accident, you became suddenly demented (or gradually with Alzheimer's), what might you want your loved ones to do? Is there a continuum of loss of mental function that you would be willing to tolerate? If you became belligerent and required restraints, would psychiatric hospitalization be in order, or would you prefer psychotropic medication if that would sedate you? What if you had to be restrained to be fed?

Coma: If you are in a coma, how long should your family wait to change the goal of treatment to comfort only? A neurologist can help determine these time parameters, as they are fairly well defined, depending on what part of the brain is affected. If you are found to have been without oxygen to your brain for over ten minutes, from which meaningful recovery is unlikely, when is it okay to discontinue all but comfort care?

PVS: If you are in a permanent vegetative state, perhaps able to track with your eyes but without cognition, when can your family change the goal to comfort? What if you can swallow some small amounts of food and water but have to have supplementation from artificial nutrition and hydration tubes to maintain a caloric intake that will sustain you?

Other Conditions

In what other scenarios would you want interventions ceased and comfort increased? When would you want everything continued? Again this discussion is not definitive, it does not mean that the person making the decisions is obligated to act immediately. In fact, your discussions should be considered broad brush guidelines to be followed after gathering data and opinions from the best medical sources available. Enough time should be allowed for decisions to be made carefully, possibly with the consultation of an ethics committee if there is disagreement or uncertainty about options, or if the decision makers simply want the opinion of those who are not directly involved with the patient.

Advance Directives

Patients and family members need to fill out a Living Will, Durable Power of Attorney for Healthcare, Organ Donor Card, or Out Of Hospital DNR (if appropriate). Make copies and distribute them to everyone who might be involved in your end-of-life treatment decisions: physicians, attorneys, clergy, next of kin. Choose the decision maker very carefully for your Durable Power of Attorney for Healthcare, and make certain you have discussed the scenarios and guidelines in as much detail as possible. This person is being asked to be *you* when you can't be.

Legal Documents

Consult your attorney to make sure that all your legal affairs are in order so that nobody is stuck in a court dilemma unable to pay your bills or receive your inheritance. Depending on the situation, a will may save the survivors time in Probate Court.

Unfinished Business

Are there people you need to talk with or want to have visit you? Nothing is guaranteed for you or them, so call them up, e-mail them, send them a fax or a letter. If they can't or won't come to you, finish the business from your side as best you can and end with your blessing.

Update

Mark your calendar as a reminder to update your checklist of issues. Some things may change based on people moving or relationships changing.

Caregivers

It is extremely important for caregivers of dying patients to examine their own deaths and consider their own potential end-of-life treatment decisions. Studies show that if I have not developed some level of decreased anxiety or peace about my own death, then I may not want the patient to talk about his or her issues and decisions, or worse, I may, through my actions or language, nudge the patient into making a treatment decision that makes *me* feel comfortable instead of focusing on the needs and wishes of the patient.

It's All about Perspective

A disciple went to his yogi master one day asking for the secret to enlightenment. The master told him to repeat the following mantra for four years and then return.

"When you breathe in, say the mantra Sen-Sah."

The disciple did as he was told and returned four years later.

"I think I've got it down," he said. "What next?"

The yogi master told him to stop the first mantra and repeat another one for four more years and return.

"When you breathe out, say the mantra Hoo-Mah."

Four years later the disciple returned, proud that he had followed exactly his master's directions, but slightly disillusioned.

"I did exactly as you said, master," the disciple whined, "but I have not yet attained enlightenment. What am I doing wrong?"

"Put the two mantras together for the next four years and return," the master said.

Four years later the disciple returned again, this time with the small smile of enlightenment on his face.

"It was not until just yesterday that I understood what you meant, master," the disciple said, shaking his head, laughing.

"Some people take longer than others," the yogi replied,

pleased that his disciple had finally developed Sen-sah Hoo-mah, a sense of humor.

Remember this story when you are in the midst of dealing with these issues. After all, it's only life and death. That is in fact what we do here. The function of a sense of humor is to put it all back in perspective, to remind us that life is short, to keep our unfinished business as finished as possible, and to live as much of a regret-free life as possible.

The Most Healing Thing

Some people think that humor is the most healing thing we do with each other, healing in the sense of wholeness, not necessarily cure (though Norman Cousins wrote about humor as curative in *Anatomy of an Illness*). Eric Berne, founder of transactional analysis *(I'm Okay, You're Okay)* believed that humor was the highest form of intimacy, that you really had to touch other people at a very deep level to make them laugh. Clearly, when caregivers or patients laugh about something, even things others would find abhorrent or inappropriate (perhaps especially so), healing is happening, acceptance is occurring, if just for an instant, and the present moment is being enjoyed regardless of past or future. Laughter only exists in the present moment, and in that sense it is timeless, reminding us of our own timelessness and the pleasure we experience with it. Indeed, a good death is one that follows a good life with an excellent Sen-sah Hoo-mah.

One Final Thought

Nobody has to do any of the things suggested here. It is entirely possible to have a good death without discussing any of the issues, providing that caregivers are given accurate information about the impending death or terminal condition of the patient. Many patients don't want to discuss anything.

They want to put themselves into the hands of their caretakers and assume those persons will do their best for them. And that can happen.

But I have often seen the lack of discussion or planning result in a reluctance to make decisions in a healthcare system which is terrified of litigation and uncertain about its obligation to the technological imperative. I have also seen family members make decisions too soon because they don't know the wishes of the patient or they don't understand the options available and may feel pressure from insurers seeking to contain costs. My concern throughout this book, and indeed in my career at the bedside of dying patients and their families, is that a patient's right to informed consent and autonomy must be taken seriously. We must honor the patient's definition of a good life and a good death in every way possible, often in spite of the system of administering treatment.

Winston Churchill said: "Americans can always be counted upon to do the right thing, but only after they have exhausted all of the other possibilities." For patients in terminal conditions and their families who are making end-of-life treatment decisions, we no longer have the luxury of exhausting all of the other technological and social possibilities. We must decide to do the right things *now* to meet the unmet needs of the ill and dying.

Determining those needs will require the formation of new vocabulary and the careful fashioning of national healthcare guidelines that are mercifully fair and socially just. On an individual basis, earlier and earlier intervention must be done by caregivers, families, and practitioners who are dealing with people in terminal conditions. They must raise questions regarding the patient's definition of quality of life and a good death, inform patients and their families about outcomes and options, and assure that caregivers will provide comfort and relieve suffering.

We must be aggressive healthcare activists and consumers to prevent others, ultimately legislators and insurance companies, from making our end-of-life decisions for us. Only then will we attain a good death for our patients and loved ones, and ultimately for ourselves.

GLOSSARY OF TERMS

Advance Directive These documents allow people to put in writing their wishes regarding medical treatment. Every state has them and most states honor reciprocity. They do not require an attorney and are free from any hospital or healthcare facility. They must be witnessed by persons who are not relatives, healthcare providers, or inheritors. Copies should be given to family, physician, hospital, and whoever is designated as a decision maker. Check your specific state's requirements regarding directives, as some differ in what they will allow. (See Durable Power of Attorney for Healthcare; Living Will; Out of Hospital Do Not Resuscitate Order; Organ Donor Card.)

Artificial Nutrition/Hydration Refers to the techniques used when the patient cannot take in or digest food by mouth.

1. Intravenous or I.V. Fluids such as saline (salt), electrolytes, vitamins, and medications are administered through a small tube inserted through a needle in a vein. *Peripheral* I.V.'s are located in the hand or arm or leg. A *Central Line* is inserted into the neck region.

2. Enteral Tubes Formula type fluids are administered through tubes inserted into the stomach or small intestine. A *Gastrostomy Tube* or *PEG* (Percutaneous Enterostomal Gastrostomy) is surgically inserted through the skin over the abdomen directly into the stomach and sewn in place to prevent accidental removal. A *Nasogastric Tube* is inserted through the nose and down the esophagus to the stomach. It is taped in place at the nostril. A small caliber *Doshoff Tube* is inserted through the nose and down across the stomach into the duodenum. In all three tubes, the amount and rate of fluid delivered is controlled by a mechanical pump.

3. TPN: Total Parenteral Nutrition (or Hyperalimentation) A special solution administered intravenously containing all nutrients necessary to maintain nutritional status. It is usually administered through a central line because the veins are larger and less likely to be irritated.

Artificial Ventilation Machines called Ventilators or Vents are used to assist or control breathing. Most patients are weaned or gradually removed from the vent, but some may become vent dependent and would die without it.

Baby Boomer Anyone born between 1946 and 1964.

Brain Death The absence of physiological activity in the brain stem. There are several tests for this including an electroencephalogram (EEG) and a Brain Blood Flow study in a CT Scanner. A non-functioning brain stem means the body is unable to maintain all other functions (breathing, heartbeat). The patient cannot recover and is considered legally dead.

CPR: Cardiopulmonary Resuscitation Includes pushing down hard on the chest (external chest compressions) to massage the heart and pump for it, artificial breathing techniques (mouth to mouth, bagging, intubation), medications, and possibly electrical shocks to the heart.

Code Status Identifies the kind of resuscitative actions to perform in case of a respiratory (lungs) or cardiac (heart) arrest (stoppage.) Code designations may vary between institutions, but they usually include:

1. Full Code. Complete CPR efforts will be used to resuscitate the patient, including admission to intensive care (ICU).

2. Intermediate Code. Also called Partial or Chemical code. Only medications will be given to restart the heart and/or respiratory system. No heart massage, artificial ventilation, or electrical shocks will be used.

3. No Code. Also called DNR and Comfort Code. No CPR or other interventions will be used on the patient. Comfort is the goal of treatment, and the patient usually is not in ICU.

CT or Cat Scan A computer assisted tomography machine uses radiation to see inside the body and produce a computer printout that looks like an x-ray.

DNR: Do Not Resuscitate Usually requires a physician's order in the patient's record or chart and designates that the goal for the patient is comfort care. Resuscitation attempts will not be started if the patient dies. Also called No Code or Comfort Code.

Durable Power of Attorney for Healthcare A legal document that designates an "agent" or "agents" who are empowered to make healthcare decisions when the person is unable to do so.

Ethics Committee Usually consists of a group of people from different professions and backgrounds who can help discuss difficult decisions regarding withdrawal of treatment, code status, or benefit of proposed treatments. Available in nearly every hospital.

ICU: Intensive Care Unit A special unit with advanced technology and trained staff with a very low nurse/patient ratio, often one to one. Includes Neuro Intensive Care and Neonatal Intensive Care.

Intractable Suffering Suffering that cannot be relieved by any means.

Intubation A tube is inserted into the trachea (windpipe) to provide Artificial Ventilation and to suction fluids that may accumulate and interfere with breathing. If ventilation is needed for a long period of time, a small incision may be made in the neck, into the trachea and a Tracheostomy tube inserted.

Kidney (Renal) Dialysis A dialysis (artificial kidney) machine is used in temporary or permanent kidney failure. Blood is removed from the body through an I.V. needle into a vein, circulated into the machine and cleansed, and returned through a vein.

Living Will A legal document for persons in a terminal condition to designate when to withdraw or withhold medical interventions and be permitted to die naturally.

MRI: Magnetic Resonance Imagery A huge magnet that takes x-ray-like pictures by changing the rotation of molecules in the body.

Organ Donor Card Most states permit residents to designate their preference on a driver's license about donating organs. Some require a form to be filled out before a person who is brain dead can have organs removed and transplanted into another person.

Out of Hospital Do Not Resuscitate Order: OHDNR A legal document for patients in a terminal condition who are at home or in a nursing facility and do not wish to be resuscitated. If 911 is inadvertently called, emergency medical service personnel are not required to resuscitate or transfer the person to a hospital emergency room.

PEG: Percutaneous Enterostomal Gastrostomy See Artificial Nutrition/Hydration.

PVS: Permanent Vegetative State A comatose state in which the brain stem is functioning enough to provide heartbeat and respiration.

Terminal Condition Generally refers to an incurable or irreversible condition caused by illness, disease, or injury in which the person would die within a relatively short time (six months to a year) without the provision of life sustaining treatment.

TPN: Total Parenteral Nutrition See Artificial Nutrition/Hydration.

Vasopressors Drugs used to sustain blood pressure in order to provide blood flow to critical organs.

Of Related Interest. . .

Surviving Death
A Practical Guide to Caring for the Dying & Bereaved
Charles Meyer
Meyer, a hospital chaplain, encourages people who have lost loved
ones to death to allow themselves to grieve, but then to move on
from grief. He seeks to dispel the myths surrounding care of the terminally ill, and presents a strong case for people confronting mortal-
ity while they are still able to do so. He addresses issues such as the
ethics of death (including withdrawal of life support), church teach-
ings on death, the spirituality of death, and specific advice for survivors.   ISBN: 0-89622-486-4, 144 pp, $9.95

Cancer and Faith
Reflections on Living with a Terminal Illness
John Carmody
This book contains more than 40 reflections that will inspire and
comfort the terminally ill as they deal with the reality of their illness
and ponder their future. As Eugene Kennedy says, John Carmody
"enables us to walk through the valley of the shadow without blink-
ing, but without fear as well.   ISBN: 0-89622-594-1, 160 pp, $9.95

Bereavement Ministry
A Leader's Resource Manual
Harriet Young, Director of Family Life Ministries
Diocese of Rapid City, South Dakota
Here is an all-encompassing resource manual for people who are
interested in ministering to those who suffer the loss of a loved one.
Each session contains clear guidelines for facilitators that include
welcoming remarks, the session presentation itself, and a closing
prayer. The book also provides several reproducible handouts for
participants that can be used during the session or taken home for
personal reflection.   ISBN: 0-89622-704-9, 96 pp, $19.95

Available at religious bookstores or from:

 TWENTY-THIRD PUBLICATIONS
1-800-321-0411
E-Mail:ttpubs@aol.com